Writings on Writing

Writings on Writing

A Compendium of 1209
Quotations from Authors
on Their Craft

THOMAS H. BRENNAN

McFarland & Company, Inc., Publishers
Jefferson, North Carolina, and London

The present work is a reprint of the library bound edition of Writings on Writing: A Compendium of 1209 Quotations from Authors on Their Craft, *first published in 1994 by McFarland.*

Library of Congress Cataloguing-in-Publication Data

Brennan, Thomas H., 1941–
    Writings on writing : a compendium of 1209 quotations from authors on their craft / Thomas H. Brennan.
        p.   cm.
    Includes index.

    ISBN 978-0-7864-7533-9
    softcover : acid free paper ∞

    1. Authorship — Quotations, maxims, etc.   I. Title.
PN165.B74 2013
808.88′2 — dc20   93-24477

British Library cataloguing data are available

On the cover: Vintage paper and feather quill (iStockphoto); inkwell and hand (clipart.com)

Manufactured in the United States of America

McFarland & Company, Inc., Publishers
    Box 611, Jefferson, North Carolina 28640
    www.mcfarlandpub.com

To my best friend, Ann.
The core will always be there.

CONTENTS

INTRODUCTION

I knew that there ought not to be any preface to this book, that it would spoil it, and I said so. But people would not believe me, and so here I am, despite myself, launched on a gratuitous and graceless undertaking in which I am sure to please nobody.
—Anatole France, Preface to
Jeunes Madames by Brada

I am an incurable collector. I was born with a highly activated packrat gene and it blossomed when I was a boy collecting baseball cards, first day covers, matchbooks, Popsicle sticks, and bottle tops. When my allowance was depleted I took up with pretty stones and rocks which were plentiful and free. During college I made lists of books I read, their authors and the dates I read them.

Several years ago I mysteriously began to acquire books, and at the same time I started copying into sewn marble notebooks quotations about writing. I remember one summer day distinctly. I was sitting on the shore of Loon Lake in Franklin County, New York, and reading Alice Munro's story "Meneseteung" which had been published in *The New Yorker* magazine on January 11, 1988. As I read the story about another of Munro's lovable Canadian characters I realized this fictional character was herself a writer, and her reflections about her own writing process might possibly be interpreted as Munro's own beliefs. Was Munro trying to tell us about her own experiences with writing through her fictional character? "I have delighted in verse and I have occupied myself—and sometimes allayed my griefs" (quotation number 857). Does writing assuage our griefs and ease our pain? Perhaps, and if so, I wondered, did other writers do the same? Did writers not only write but also try to tell us why? I didn't know, so I began to collect quotations to find the answer.

I had, of course, already embarked on collecting quotation books exclusively devoted to books and writing. They included *Writers on Writing* by Jon Winokur, *Shoptalk* by Donald M. Murray, *On Being a Writer* by Bill Strickland, and my favorite title, *How Many Books Do You Sell in Ohio?* by Bill Gordon. Only the latter gave more detailed information about the quotation including its source and date, and the question naturally arose as to whether the people quoted in the other books really said or wrote what was attributed to them. Thus this book was born and its purpose was to tie original source and date to all quotations.

To accomplish this I set off immediately to the bowels of libraries, to wander through the dusty fluorescent-lit stacks trying to discover what writers themselves thought of writing, and in the search for attribution I discovered the lost candy shop of my childhood. There were more quotations about writing and the process of composing than I had ever dreamed possible. All of the writers who lived and penned, it seemed, wanted not only to write but to tell us clearly why they wanted to write. Never mind that their reasons were contradictory: how hard it was, how easy it all seemed sometimes, how depressing, how liberating, how mysterious, how commonplace, how rewarding, how deleterious to body and soul. I found quotations in newspapers, novels, biographies, autobiographies, letters, short stories and essays. I marveled at how easy it was to find these gems of wisdom, and my notebooks exploded with quotations. I found both the famous writer and the unsung hack searching for the meaning of writing. Most importantly I tried to find when and where they first said it.

In my collecting I unearthed humor, depression, desire, ambition, defeat, sarcasm, and a range of other human emotions. During my collection I stumbled upon a quotation of Jack London in a book review about Upton Sinclair's *The Jungle*, and its subsequent famous usage, slightly modified by Winston Churchill. London commented in 1905 about Sinclair's book. "It is brutal with life. It is written of sweat, and blood, and groans and tears" (quotation 1057). Of all books this is true, but discoveries like this one made the collecting memorable. One assumes here that Churchill enjoyed reading Jack London so much that he absorbed his words into his own psyche. Churchill said as much in his book *My Early Life*: "Quotations when engraved upon the memory give you good thoughts" (quotation 389).

Unfortunately, I was unable to find some of my favorite quotations, and without the primary source and date I could not include them in this collection. One of these quotations is attributed to Franz Kafka. It has been translated and is noted in several quotations books. Murray's version reads, "A book should serve as the axe for the frozen sea within us," which is slightly different from Charles Neider's epigraph in his book *The Frozen Sea*, which is rendered, "A book must be the ax for the frozen sea within us." Kafka most probably said it or wrote it, but sadly I could not find the original source for attribution.

My collection contains over 1,200 quotations which should satisfy any inveterate quotation lover. The majority concern the process of writing, but others reflect about books, book collectors, language, libraries, and other first cousins of writing. I only stopped because the manuscript was due at the publisher, but like any hardened collector I continue my search. I hope that you, the reader, enjoy them, and that they assist you, the writer, to discover for yourself the reasons why you write.

There are many people to thank for eagerly answering my questions and suggesting further strategies for research, but you the reader will know none of them by name. They all have one thing in common — they care about books, cherish writing, and were thrilled to help me learn more about books and writing. They are called librarians, but in reality they are lovers of books and writing.

Thomas H. Brennan
September 17, 1993

THE QUOTATIONS

• Autobiography/Biography •

1. Oscar Wilde has said somewhere that, among the friends of a great man, as among the Apostles, there is always a Judas. It is he who writes his biography.
— TOM ANTONGINI, *D'Annunzio*, 1938

2. Neither the biographer nor the autobiographer is entitled to impose a stylish shape on lived experience, as the novelist does. Their job is to record, to take into account the chaos and mystery of human nature, to preserve a reverence for life itself.
— ANN ARENSBERG, *New York Times Book Review*, August 26, 1990

3. Not every great writer earns a great biography.
— JAMES ATLAS, "Choosing a Life," *New York Times*, January 13, 1991

4. "A well written life is almost as rare as a well spent one." If that is true of lives, it is even truer of autobiographies.
— WILLIAM BARCLAY, commenting on an unidentified quotation used by Margot Asgruth in *A Spiritual Biography (Testament of Faith)*, 1975

5. Biography is different from Geography. Geography is about maps while Biography deals with chaps.
— EDMUND CLERIHEW BENTLEY, "Dictionary of Biography" from *The First Clerihews*, 1982

6. Autobiography is often an excuse for not going on any more . . . my book is my blood.
— HORTENSE CALISHER, *Herself*, 1972

7. An author by profession had need narrowly to watch his pen, lest a line should escape it which by possibility may do mischief, when he has been long dead and buried.
— WILLIAM COWPER, letter, August 16, 1789

8. **Question:** Is biography really an art or is it, in fact, a structural piecing together of fragments — a form of carpentry?
Answer: There is carpentry involved, of course, but what I was

doing was finding a form to suit my materials as I went along, having from the first given myself a large design. The moment you start shaping a biography, it becomes more than a mere assemblage of facts, mere use of lumber and nails—you are creating a work of art. I think I was performing like a dramaticist when I planted my pistols ahead of time, and like a novelist when I did a flashback—incorporating retrospective chapters as I moved from theme to theme, character to character, showing the hero making mistakes and correcting them, facing adversity and learning from experience, growing older and having his particular kind of artistic and intellectual adventures. . . . All this required what I like to call the biographical imagination, the imagination of form. As biographers, we are not allowed to imagine our facts. . . . The difference between a novelist and a biographer resides in the biographies having to master a narrative of inquiry. Biography has to explain and examine the evidence.

—LEON EDEL, "Writers at Work,"
Paris Review Interviews, 8th Series, 1988

9. The biographer may be as imaginative as he pleases—the more imaginative the better—in the way in which he brings together his materials, but he must not imagine the materials.

—LEON EDEL, *Literary Biography*, 1957

10. The next thing most like living one's life over again seems to be a recollection of that life, and to make that recollection as durable as possible by putting it down in writing.

—BENJAMIN FRANKLIN, *Autobiography*, 1771

11. You have but two subjects, yourself and me.

—SAMUEL JOHNSON, about James Boswell,
related by Mark Schorer, *The Burdens of Biography*,
Hopewood Lecture, 1962

12. I have often thought that there has rarely passed a life of which a judicious and faithful narrative would not be useful.

—SAMUEL JOHNSON, *The Rambler*, No. 60,
Saturday, October 13, 1750

13. Biography has often been allotted to writers who seem very little acquainted with the nature of their task, or very negligent about the performance.

—SAMUEL JOHNSON, *The Rambler*, No. 60,
Saturday, October 13, 1750

14. His diaries became not a mere exercise in self-portraiture, but a faithful re-creation of an age.
— JOHN F. KENNEDY, on John Adams,
American Historical Review, January 1963

15. To write one's memoirs before one has reached the age of fifty may seem a premature and somewhat presumptuous undertaking.
— ARTHUR KOESTLER, AUTHOR'S NOTE TO
The Invisible Writing, December 31, 1953

16. It would be foolish to blame biographers for failing to illuminate a process so complex and mysterious as the act of composition.
— ERICH LEINSDORF, *The Composer's Advocate,* 1981

17. It's frightening to think someone you engage as your cook-housekeeper might write an autobiographical novel based on her stay in the house.
— JOE ORTON, diary, July 4, 1967

18. It's also true that biographers, like the rest of us, are drawn to colorful stories — suicide, madness, sex, outrageous behavior.
— KATHA POLLETT, *New York Times Book Review,* August 26, 1990

19. [Dorothy Parker's] unexpected comment was: "Rather than write my life story I would cut my throat with a dull knife." Then she reflected, "But let's face it friend; this is something you could pull off. At least your autobiography would be different. For once we wouldn't have a man blaming his failures on an unhappy childhood. . . . You're a horribly normal man. I doubt if many horrible normal men write their autobiographies.
"Well, I might try it," I said doubtfully, "but one thing troubles me. A man who writes his autobiography ought to have a few lessons to teach. . . ."
"Skip the lessons and just write about what happened to you," she observed. And that is what I have done.
— QUENTIN REYNOLDS, *By Quentin Reynolds,* 1963

20. Most biographies are not written with the sole object of producing an interesting book. In some cases the author's main purpose seems to be to write what would please the deceased. In others the biography is written to please his relatives by whom it has been commissioned.
— LORD RIDDELL, *More Things That Matter,* 1925

21. The key to successful biography lies in the depth of a writer's empathy.

— JUDITH SHULEVITZ, on Philip Hoare,
New York Times, February 3, 1991

22. A book is at best a poor contrivance to catch a life in.

— PAGE SMITH, *John Adams*, 1962

23. There are still further reasons which induce me to write this book. In numerous interviews I have given my thoughts, my words, and even facts have often been disfigured.

— IGOR STRAVINSKY, *An Autobiography*, 1936

24. Every man's life may be best written by himself.

— SAMUEL BOSWELL, *Life of Samuel Johnson*, 1791

• Books •

25. If everybody could read all the books that have ever been published and still have time left over to lead a normal life devoted to other interests, there would be little need for universities.

— LYMAN ABBOTT, *The Guide to Reading*, 1924

26. Young gentlemen take every evening in this town, playing cards, drinking punch and wine, smoking tobacco, swearing and c.[ursing] while 100 of the best books lie on the shelves, desks, and chairs, in the same room.

— JOHN ADAMS, diary, February 11, 1759

27. I suppose every one who travels daily by bus, tram or train has noticed the keen and growing competition between the newspaper and the book. So far the former has won easily. Six passengers are reading the daily for everyone reading the novel.

— JOHN ADAMSON, "Wild and Whirling Words,"
in *Externals and Essentials*, 1933

28. French novels with metaphysical or psychological prefaces are always certain to be particularly indecent.

— THOMAS BAILEY ALDRICH,
Ponkapog Papers, 1902

29. Is there anything more interesting than browsing around a dusty old bookshop, especially in Italy? Browsolatry is, in fact, the first step in bookish adventure.

— RUDOLPH ALTROCCHI, *Sleuthing in the Stacks*, 1944

30. Burton Rascoe told me yesterday that *Winesburg* was a best seller in Chicago this week. My God, suppose you and I should make some money.

— SHERWOOD ANDERSON, letter
to Ben Huebsch, June 14, 1919

31. It is a curious mania (book collecting) instantly understood by every other collector and almost incomprehensible to the uncontaminated.

— LOUIS AUCHINCLOSS, *A Writer's Capital*, 1974

32. Attacking bad books is not only a waste of time but also bad for the character.

— W. H. AUDEN, "Reading," *The Dyer's Hand*, 1962

33. God's knowledge ... is the book of life.

— ST. AUGUSTINE, *City of God*, xx, 15

34. Some books are to be tasted, others to be swallowed, and some few to be chewed and digested.

— FRANCIS BACON, "On Studies," 1625

35. Reading maketh a full man, conference a ready man, and writing an exact man.

— FRANCIS BACON, "On Studies," 1625

36. God be thanked for books! They are the voices of the distant and the dead.

— JAMES BALDWIN, *The Book-Lover*, 1888

37. The failure of the protest novel lies in its rejection of life, the human being, the denial of his beauty, dread, power.

— JAMES BALDWIN, *Partisan Review*, June 1949

38. The history that lies inert in unread books does no work in the world.

— CARL BECKER, *American Historical Review*,
Vol. xxxviii, No. 2, January 1932

39. There are too many men who have a dyspepsia of books.
— HENRY WARD BEECHER,
Notes from Plymouth Pulpit, 1865

40. It was kind of you to think of sending me a copy of your new book. It would have been kinder still to think again and abandon that project.
— MAX BEERBOHM, *How Shall I Word It?* 1910

41. The two finest rules for an inexperienced book-collector are:
1. Never buy a book that you don't believe you want to read.
2. Never read a book that you haven't bought.
— ARNOLD BENNETT, "Buying and Reading Books"
in *Things That Have Interested Me*, 1926

42. Schoolbooks are popular only in the sense that taxes are popular.
— ARNOLD BENNETT, "Buying and Reading Books"
in *Things That Have Interested Me*, 1926

43. I am not aware that novels are more trashy than other forms of literature.
— ARNOLD BENNETT, "Buying and Reading Books"
in *Things That Have Interested Me*, 1926

44. As a rule people don't collect books; they let books collect themselves.
— ARNOLD BENNETT, "Buying and Reading Books"
in *Things That Have Interested Me*, 1926

45. The man who adds the life of books to the actual life of everyday lives the life of the whole race. The man without books lives only the life of one individual.
— JESSIE LEE BENNETT, *What Books Can Do for You*, 1923

46. The book is the thing. Literature was meant to give pleasure, to excite interest, to banish solitude, to make the fireside more attractive than the tavern, to give joy to those who are still capable of joy, and — why should we not admit it? — to drug sorrow and divert thought.
— AUGUSTINE BIRRELL, Introduction to
Boswell's Life of Johnson, 1896

47. It is strange how often men and women who write books forget all about the men and women who occasionally read them, a forgetful folly akin to that of the man who, having challenged a bruiser to engage in fisticuffs, lays down a plan of attack, but forgets to remember that his opponent is not likely to stand still all the time. Nowadays many readers are at least as clever as most authors. . . . Anyone who begins writing about himself runs a risk beyond that of his publishers; for, self-deluded as he may be about his character, or however skillful he thinks he has been in concealing it — out the truth will come. . . . Unless a book reveals a character behind it, good or bad, it is a thing of naught. Do you wish your real character to be self-revealed? If so, try your hand at autobiography.

—AUGUSTINE BIRRELL, *Et Cetera*, 1930

48. A book is not a bar of soap.
—JEANNE BLUMBERG, Gannett Westchester Newspapers, December 16, 1990

49. Without books we might be tempted to believe that our civilization was born yesterday — or when the latest newsmagazine went to press. The very omnipresence of books leads us to underestimate their power and influence.
—DANIEL J. BOORSTIN, *Books in Our Future*, 1984

50. We are often told that we are what we eat. In our world since the printing press it might be more accurate to say we are what we read. How each of us digests what we read is a mystery. And what people really read is sometimes as puzzling as what they really think.
—DANIEL J. BOORSTIN, Introduction to *A Memoir* by Louis L'Amour, 1989

51. Books are messengers of freedom. They can be hidden under a mattress or smuggled into slave nations.
—DANIEL J. BOORSTIN, *Books in Our Future*, 1984

52. The study of the novel has become one of the great growth industries of modern criticism.
—MALCOLM BRADBURY, *Possibilities*, 1973

53. A novel must be something, before it can begin to mean anything.
—MALCOLM BRADBURY, quoting Alain Robbe-Grillet in *Possibilities*, 1973

54. A short story is usually a collision, abrupt, and over in a few hours. A novel grows more slowly until suddenly it is there. My short stories hit and run, astonishing me with the way they grab, shake me, and let me go. My novels invariably surprise me in another way, with the fact they have been around so long and I have been blind to the fact of their existence.

— RAY BRADBURY, Introduction to *Fahrenheit 451*, 1966

55. You see my problem was Edgar Rice Burroughs and Tarzan and John Carter, Warlord of Mars. Problem, you ask. That doesn't sound like much of a problem. Oh, but it was. You see, I couldn't stop reading those books.

— RAY BRADBURY, Introduction to
Edgar Rice Burroughs by Irwin Porges, May 8, 1975

56. The emergence of the novel as a "character art" very likely reflects the increase in self-consciousness that has been part of the development of our civilization.

— JEROME BRUNER, *On Knowing*, 1962

57. This is an erotic novel, not a pornographic one. There is, after all, a difference.

— ANTHONY BURGESS, on Mario Vargas Llosa's novel
In Praise of the Stepmother in *The New York Times
Book Review*, October 14, 1990

58. If I had to sell something for a living let me say at once that I would rather sell books than anything else.

— MARTIN BURRELL, *Crumbs Are Also Bread*, 1934

59. I am getting tired of reading current novels, and I do not think I am alone in that.

— DOUGLAS BUSH, "Sex in the Modern Novel,"
Atlantic Monthly, January 1959

60. I must tell you that as each book was published, and indeed each magazine tale, I have regularly burned the manuscript. . . . I am still almost sure all manuscripts ought to be burned.

— JAMES BRANCH CABELL,
letter to Burton Rascoe, March 13, 1918

61. I don't know how many books on *Hamlet* there are that set out to elucidate its mysteries.

— JOHN CAGE, *X: Writings '79–'82*

62. Nothing comes whole to a reviewer. Half of every book must elude him, and the other half he must compress into snappy phrases.
— HENRY SEIDAL CANBY, *Definitions*, 1922

63. Looking back on a world and wasted life, I realize that I have especially sinned in neglecting to read novels.
— G. K. CHESTERTON, "On Philosophy Versus Fiction" in *All Is Grist*, 1932

64. Let others be ashamed who have so buried themselves in books that they can offer nothing for the common enjoyment.
— CICERO, "In Defense of the Poet Archias," 62 B.C.

65. The theory is that if a famous author says another author is terrific, the public, sheeplike, will line up and buy the book in question.
— WILLIAM COLE, *New York Times Book Review*, July 23, 1978

66. I would prefer . . . no new novels to be published for three years, their sale forbidden . . . and nobody under thirty should be allowed to write one.
— CYRIL CONNOLLY, *The Condemned Playground*, 1944

67. It has been said a long time ago that books have their fate. They have, and it is very much like the destiny of man. They share with us the great incertitudes of ignominy or glory — of severe justice and senseless persecution — the shame of undeserved success. Of all the inanimate objects, of all men's creations, books are nearest to us, for they contain our very thought, our ambitions, our indignations, our illusions, our fidelity to truth, and our persistent leaning toward error. But most of all they resemble us in their precarious hold on life. . . . Of all books, novels . . . make a serious claim on our compassions. The art of the novelist is simple. At the same time it is the most elusive of all creative arts, the most liable to be obscured.
— JOSEPH CONRAD, *Notes of Life and Letters*, 1921

68. I don't remember any child's book; I don't think I ever read any.
— JOSEPH CONRAD, *T.P.'s Weekly of London*, January 9, 1903

69. I am now wrestling — at the closest of quarters — with chapter xxiii of my new book. Then comes chapter xxiv and then — the deluge. The deluge of doubts, remorse, regrets and fear.
— JOSEPH CONRAD, Letter to Mademoiselle Briquel, July 14, 1985

70. A sense of regret [cannot] be dismissed for the pleasant days when the public sought and found the best of entertainment in reading books.
—THOMAS B. COSTAIN, A Word of
Explanation in *Read with Me*, 1965

71. Sooner or later the life of our time is summarized in its books.
—MALCOLM COWLEY, *Books That
Changed Our Minds*, 1938

72. As far as books are concerned I am *totus teres atque rotundus* and may set fortune at defiance.
—WILLIAM COWPER, letter, May 8, 1788

73. It would be a strange writer who didn't think it hard that books should sell a lot, but not his.
—JAMES COZZENS, *Notebooks*, November 4, 1961

74. There is no surer oblivion than that which awaits one whose name is recorded in a book that undertakes to tell all.
—SAMUEL MCCHORD CROTHERS, *The Gentle Reader*, 1903

75. Modern historical novels have spread the delusion that in the seventeenth and eighteenth centuries people gave all their time to sex, and in the nineteenth century devoted themselves wholly to sex and adventures, such as building railroads. But previous to the seventeenth century people had neither sex nor railroads, and were consequently of no interest to anyone, even themselves.
—ROBERTSON DAVIES, *The Papers of Samuel Marshbanks*, 1986

76. Beside a library, how poor are all the other greatest deeds of man.
—THOMAS DAVIS, *Essay on Study*, 1845

77. Happiest is he who judges and knows books.
—THOMAS DAVIS, *Essay on Study*, 1845

78. In books I find the dead as if they were alive.
—RICHARD DE BURY, "The Love of Books,"
The Philobiblon, 1473

79. The purpose of fiction is still, as it was to Joseph Conrad, to make the reader see.
—PETER DEVRIES, quoted in *Without a Stitch in Time*, 1972

80. In reading a novel, even one written by an expert craftsman, one may get the feeling early in the story that the hero or heroine is doomed, doomed not by anything inherent in situations and character but by the intent of the author who makes the character a puppet to set forth his own cherished idea. The painful feeling that results is resented not because it is painful but because it is foisted upon us by something that we feel comes from outside the movement of the subject matter.
— JOHN DEWEY, *Art as Experience*, 1934

81. Like a man a book should have an individuality of its own.
— THOMAS H. DICKERSON, *The Making of American Literature*, 1932

82. You must admit it's the most tedious job in the world reading all the tedious books which come out.
— DENIS DIDEROT, Letter to Sophie Volland, August 31, 1769

83. I admire all his books; it is astonishing what a gallery of characters he has, unlike any modern author almost — perhaps Tolstoy approaches it.
— ISAK DINESEN, concerning Charles Dickens, *Letters from Africa*, April 13, 1930

84. We become so used to having the famous books around most of the time we look at them as though they were statues of generals in public parks.
— GEORGE P. ELLIOT, *Wonder for Huckleberry Finn*, 1958

85. Books ruin women's wits — which are none too plentiful anyway.
— DESIDERIUS ERASMUS, *The Colloquies*, 1516

86. Two forbidden pages out of some tawdry "sex book," read when one was eleven, may have had more influence on one than all the works of Freud.
— CLIFTON FADIMAN, *Books That Changed Our Minds*, 1938

87. Books do actually consume air and exhale perfumes.
— EUGENE FIELD, *Love Affairs of a Bibliomaniac*, 1897

88. This book is the literary equivalent of a sandwich without bread.
— MALCOLM FORBES, JR., on Anne Fisher's *Wall Street Women*, in *The New York Times Book Review*, February 4, 1990

89. I would define a book as a work of witchcraft from which there escapes all sorts of images which disturb people's minds and change their hearts.
— ANATOLE FRANCE, *On Life and Letters*, First Series, 1911

90. Books are the opium of the West. They devour us. A day will come when we shall all be librarians and that will end it all.
— ANATOLE FRANCE, *On Life and Letters*, First Series, 1911

91. There is no true love without some sensuality. One is not happy in books unless one loves to caress them.
— ANATOLE FRANCE, *One Life and Letters*, Second Series, 1914

92. I haven't written for a few days, because I wanted first of all to think about my diary. It's an odd idea for someone like me to keep a diary; not only because I have never done so before but because it seems to me that neither I — nor for that matter anyone else — will be interested in the unbosomings of a thirteen year old school girl. Still, what does that matter? I want to write, but more than that, I want to bring out all kinds of things that lie buried deep in my heart.

There is a saying that "paper is more patient than man" . . . there is no doubt that paper is patient and I don't intend to show this cardboard-covered notebook, bearing the proud name of "diary" to anyone, unless I find a real friend, boy or girl, probably nobody cares. And now I come to the root of the matter, the reason for my starting a diary: it is that I have no such real friend.
— ANNE FRANK, *The Diary of a Young Girl*, 1947

93. I like rereading books, too. I don't trust folk who don't re-read. . . . What you've got to teach people is to read slowly.
— ROBERT FROST, quoted by Octavio Paz in
Poets and Others, June 1945

94. Should you acquire a habit of making good books your companions they will form your minds to a love of better pleasures.
— MARGARET FULLER, letter to the
women at Sing Sing, November 1844

95. To print and sell them (two of my books) openly seemed to be the easiest way of offering civil disobedience.
— MOHANDAS GANDHI, *Autobiography*, 1927–1929

96. We never thought of making our books and poems public, even in the family; they were written because they must be and entirely for ourselves.

—JON AND RUMER GODDEN, *Two Under the Indian Sun*, 1966

97. Browse through the library of any writer or exemplary teacher and you will find the leaves of the book dog-eared and scribbled notations in all the margins. No one interested in what an author is saying should read without pencil in hand.

—HARRY GOLDEN, *So What Else Is New*, 1964

98. Books do not make life easier or more simple, but harder and more interesting.

—HARRY GOLDEN, *So What Else Is New*, 1964

99. Emperor: Poems? You are a poet? That is quite incredible.
Phanodes: Mamillius wrote the lines.
Emperor: I might have known. Sophocles—Aeschylus—How well read the boy is!
Phanodes: This will make him famous. Read both papers, Caesar, for they are exactly the same. I have invented a cheap and noiseless method of multiplying books. I call it printing.
Emperor: Printing?
Phanodes: Think. How many books of mathematics are irretrievably lost that this invention would have saved for us? How much astronomy, medicine if you will—husbandry, essential skills—
Emperor: But this is another pressure cooker!
Phanodes: By this method a man and a boy could make a thousand copies of a book in a day.
Emperor: We could give away a hundred thousand copies of the works of Homer.
Phanodes: A million if you will.
Emperor: A poet will sell his verses by the sack, like vegetables— "Buy my fine ripe odes."
Phanodes: A public library in every town!

—WILLIAM GOLDING, *The Brass Butterfly*, 1958

100. There are some characters in books who live their own abundant life beyond the threshold of our business of moral judgments. Here we are, they seem to say, and now what are you going to make of us?

—WILLIAM GOLDING, "Islands in Books" in *The Hot Gates*, 1966

101. A book that wins a prize wins readers.

—BESSIE GRAHAM, *Famous Literary Prizes*, 1939

102. The book tour is a staple of modern literary life.
—BOB GREEN, "Book 'Em," *Esquire*, March 1985

103. First of all reading wisely is obviously to be able to select and read only good books, and to leave the bad ones aside.
—MASON W. GROSS, speech, National Book Committee, November 18, 1959

104. It [the diary] was begun without a thought of anybody else reading it. But, what with my later history and all that has been said and written about me, the situation has changed. These entries provide the only true "profile" that can be drawn. That is why, during recent years, I have reckoned with the possibility of publication, though I have continued to write for myself, not for the public.

If you find them worth publishing, you have my permission to do so—as a sort of white book concerning my negotiations with myself—and with God.
—DAG HAMMARSKJÖLD, *Markings*, 1965

105. A book is good, bad or medium for me, and I usually don't know the reasons why.
—LILLIAN HELLMAN, *An Unfinished Woman*, 1969

106. Forgotten books are being rediscovered all the time.
—GERALD HOWARD, *New York Times Book Review*, December 23, 1990

107. Let criticism do what it may, writers will write, printers will print, and the world will inevitably be overstocked with good books.
—WASHINGTON IRVING, "The Mutability of Literature," from *The Sketch Book of Geoffrey Crayon, Gent.*, 1832

108. Write it before them on a tablet, and inscribe it in a book, that it may be for the time to come as a witness for ever.
—ISAIAH 30:8

109. And because there is no human contact, you depend on books. . . . The only friend I had was a book. Sometimes I'd find myself talking out loud to the author. . . . When I'm asleep at night, I still find myself talking to those guys.
—GEORGE JACKSON, on solitary confinement, *Blood in My Eye*, February 1972

110. If books were judged by the bad uses man can put them to, what book has been more misused than the Bible.
—WALTER KAUFMAN, quoting Maritain in *The Portable Nietzsche*, 1954

111. He wrote the book in five months, beginning in May and ending in late October 1938, writing in longhand and producing 2,000 words a day, the equivalent of seven double-spaced typed pages, and enormous output for any writer, and ultimately a daily tour de force.
—WILLIAM KENNEDY, on John Steinbeck, *New York Times*, April 9, 1989

112. There is no point in pretending that this is not going to be an argumentative book.
—WALTER KERR, Introduction to *How Not to Write a Play*, 1955

113. When I was a child, I liked to read. I loved *Jane Eyre* especially and read it over and over. I didn't know anyone else who liked to read except my mother, and it got me into a lot of trouble because it made me into a thief and a liar. I stole books, and I stole money to buy them. . . . Books brought me the greatest satisfaction. Just to be alone, reading, under the house, with lizards and spiders running around.
—JAMICA KINCAID, *New York Times Interview*, August 19, 1990

114. Persistent readers of novels will usually confess that what began as a passion tends to end as a habit.
—JOSEPH WOOD KRUTCH, "The Nation,"
printed in *The College Book of Essays*, 1939

115. To make a book is as much a trade as to make a clock; something more than intelligence is required to become an author.
—LA BRUYÈRE, *Characters*, 1688

116. A printing press can deliver edifying books one day and shilling shockers the next. It pays no attention to such small matters. And the reader of either product will not therefore sense anything unsavory.
—PÄR LAGERHVIST, *Modern Theater*, 1918

117. Give me a thrill, says the reader,
      Give me a kick;
      I don't care how you succeed, or
      What subject you pick.
      Choose something you know all about
      That'll sound like real life.
—PHILIP LARKIN, *Fiction and the Reading Public*, February 1950

118. If you want to get ahead in this world, get a lawyer—not a book.
—FRAN LEBOWITZ, *Metropolitan Life*, 1974–1978

119. By their very nature the formative books in the history of thought are those that break the boundary lines of thought.
—MAX LERNER, *Important Books of the Last One Hundred Years*, 1939

120. When a book and a head collide and a hollow sound is heard, isn't it always the fault of the book?
—GEORGE CHRISTOPHER LICHTENBERG, *The Notebook*, 1764–1799

121. There can hardly be a stranger commodity in the world than books. Printed by people who don't understand them: sold by people who don't understand them: bound, criticized, and read by people who don't understand them: and now even written by people who don't understand them.
—GEORGE CHRISTOPHER LICTENBERG, *The Notebook*, 1764–1799

122. Among the greatest discoveries that the human mind has come upon in recent times belongs, I suppose, the art of judging books without having read them.
—GEORGE CHRISTOPHER LICHTENBERG, *The Notebook*, 1764–1799

123. A book is a mirror: if an ass peers into it you can't expect an apostle to look out.
—GEORGE CHRISTOPHER LICTENBERG, *The Notebook*, 1764–1799

124. The opening of a free, public library, then, is a most important event in the history of any town.
—JAMES RUSSELL LOWELL, *Books and Libraries*, December 22, 1885

125. It seemed good to me also, having followed all things closely for some time past, to write an orderly account for you.
—LUKE 1:3

126. His book on Ethics is worse than any other book.
—MARTIN LUTHER on Aristotle's *Ethics*, "An Appeal to the Ruling Class," 1520

127. For neither many books nor much reading make a man learned.
— MARTIN LUTHER, "An Appeal to the Ruling Class," 1520

128. This book of mine is what you are looking for and eagerly begin to read.
— LUXORIUS, Poem 2, Sixth century

129. The book and the author are considered as one. To admire the book is to admire the author.
— THOMAS MACAULAY, Crocker's edition of
Boswell's Life of Johnson, September 1831

130. A successful book cannot venture to be more than ten per cent new.
— DWIGHT MACDONALD, "Running It Up the Totem Pole"
in *McLuhan: Pro and Con*, 1968

131. The distich writer seeks to please
By being brief and quick
But what's the use of brevity
In a book three inches thick.
— MARTIAL, *Epigrams*, viii. 29, 80 A.D.

132. Books are no longer the scarce fruit of solemn and protracted thought.
— HARRIET MARTINEAU, *Autobiography*, 1821

133. All sacred books are exclusive. They tolerate no rivals . . . no book can be a holy Bible that is not also the only Bible.
— FREDERIC ROWLAND MARVIN,
The Companionship of Books, 1905

134. The writing of a novel has become problematic today. It is still possible to write novels . . . real novels — not fairy tales or fables or romances or contes philosophiques, and I mean novels of high order, like *War and Peace,* or *Middlemarch,* or *Ulysses* or the novels of Dickens, Dostoevsky, or Proust. The manufacture of second-rate novels, or, rather, of facsimiles of the novel, is in no state of crisis. . . . But almost no writer in the West of any consequence, let us say since the death of Thomas Mann, has been able to write a true novel; the exception is Faulkner.
— MARY MCCARTHY, *On the Contrary: Articles of Belief 1946–1961*

135. They should also give me 1 doz. copies of the book.... The sooner the thing is printed and published the better. The "season" will make little or no difference, I fancy, in this case. After printing don't let the book hang back.
— HERMAN MELVILLE, Memorandum for Allan (Melville) Concerning the Publication of *My Verses,* June 1, 1860

136. If I undertook to tell you the effect it had upon me my talk would sound frantic, and even delirious. Its impact was genuinely terrific. I had not gone further than the first impressionable chapter before I realized, child though I was, that I had entered a domain of new and gorgeous wonders.
— H. L. MENCKEN, *Happy Days 1880–1892*

137. Burn proofs when read. You shall have the book on publication.
— GEORGE MEREDITH, letter to Lady Ulrica Duncombe, February 4, 1902

138. Who kills a man kills a reasonable creature, God's image; but he who destroys a good book, kills reason itself, kills the image of God.
— JOHN MILTON, *Areopagitica,* November 24, 1644

139. A good book is the precious life blood of a master-spirit.
— JOHN MILTON, *Areopagitica,* November 24, 1644

140. I am now so much alone, I have leisure to pass whole days in reading.
— (LADY) MARY WORTLEY MONTAGU, letter to Anne Wortley, August 8, 1709

141. I do not take much to modern books, because the ancient ones seem to me fuller and stronger.
— MONTAIGNE, *On Books,* 1578

142. A witty epigram of the Spanish poet contains this thought: "To live, a book must have genius."
— SIR THOMAS MORE, Latin Epigrams, #226, circa 1509

143. The book, if read, would secure the nation's happiness.
— SIR THOMAS MORE, on Thomas à Kempis' *The Following of Christ,* letter to Erasmus, March 1526

144. What do we need with all those law books? Practically all the cases are hypothetical and do not conform to the general rule.

—MONTESQUIEU, *The Persian Letters*, 1721

145. How curious that the writings which inspire revolutionary action are almost uniformly boring as hell.

—MALCOLM MUGGERIDGE, *Esquire*, August 1967

146. You read my book as if it were yours;
The way you read it, I wish it were.

—PHILIP MURRAY, *Poems After Martial*, 1967

147. What's the good of brevity
If it makes a book.

—PHILIP MURRAY, *Poems After Martial*, 1967

148. Never let it be said that you allowed a book about books to usurp the power of the books themselves.

—DANIEL J. O'NEILL, epigraph in *A Book About Books*, 1936

149. Where is your book? We've never received one. Do you mean to say I'm going to have to buy it?

—EUGENE O'NEILL, letter to
George Jean Nathan, November 12, 1929

150. Who could list ten books for special praises
When books grew wild like buttercups and daisies?

—OGDEN NASH, *You Can't Get There from Here*, 1957

151. The first thing to do is to make absolutely sure that you really do like reading. The thing is supposed to be, and often is, a pleasure; there is no possible reason why it should be elevated into a duty. You should begin by reading ill-written books and those which your more literate friends decry. Well-written books often require some effort on the part of the reader.

—HAROLD NICOLSON, "How to Read Books" from *Small Talk*, 1937

152. What most often makes my books obscure—there is in me a distrust of dialectic, even of reasons.

—FRIEDRICH NIETZSCHE, letter to Georg Brandis, December 2, 1887

153. A man (or a woman) is the most interesting thing in the world; and next is a book, which enables one to get at the heart of the mystery.

—A. EDWARD NEWTON, *The Amenities of Book-Collecting*, 1918

154. There are always more books to condemn than to praise.
— PETER S. PRESCOTT, *Soundings*, 1972

155. It is good fiction, so largely ignored now, that brings us so much closer to the real facts.
— J. B. PRIESTLEY, "Fact or Fiction?," *New Statesman*, January 6, 1967

156. There are books which I couldn't understand and which I like now.
— MARCEL PROUST, letter to Leon Daudet, February 1899

157. In most of our childhoods there have been those books beloved, not because they are marvelous children's books, but because they are marvelous books.
— ANNA QUINDLEN, *New York Times Book Review*, March 3, 1991

158. [We] have always maintained with Macaulay that we would rather be a poor man with books than a great king without though luckily . . . such a choice has never been offered.
— AGNUS REPPLIER, *Book and Men*, 1888

159. Books bring with them detachment and a critical attitude that is not possible in a society dependent on the spoken word.
— DAVID RIESMAN, "Oral Tradition, Written Word, Screen Image" in *Abundance for What?*, 1964

160. Its publishing history shows what a glorious nut book people can get in when they lost sight of what writing is supposed to be.
— ROGER ROSENBLATT, on Bret Ellis' book *American Psycho* in *New York Times Book Review*, November 16, 1990

161. Looking over a huge catalogue of new books, one might weep at thinking that, when ten years have passed, not one of them will be heard of . . . hence, in regard to reading, it is a very important thing to be able to refrain. . . . The man who writes for fools is always sure of a large audience.
— ARTHUR SCHOPENHAUER, "On Books and Reading" in *The Art of Literature*, 1818

162. What we call the taste of the age, in books as in anything else, naturally influences more or less those who belong to that age.
— SIR WALTER SCOTT, "Of the Hue That Is Blue," *The Private Letter-Books*, September 4, 1826

163. If used right, books . . . do not have to be a substitute for our own creative activity.
—PETE SEEGER, *The Extroduction of Henscratches and Flyspecks*, 1973

164. This reading of many authors and all sorts of books may mean a measure of instability and vagabondage.
—SENECA, letter to Lucilius, on reading many books

165. A thousand books my library contains;
And all are printed, it seems to me, with brains.
Mine are so few I scratch in thought my head
For just a hundred of the lot I've read.
—ROBERT SERVICE, *Rhymes for My Rags*, 1956

166. Everything in the world exists in order that it may end up in a book.
—RANDALL SHORT, *New York Times*, January 27, 1991

167. Remember that the book itself is an odd object, floating in the complicated context of a writer's thoughts and feelings. A book reflects idiosyncratic decisions: what to exclude, how to interpret and translate reality.
—LINDA SIMON, *New York Times Book Review*, September 9, 1990

168. This book began, as I suspect many books do, in a conversation; or a series of conversations.
—PAGE SMITH, *As a City Upon a Hill*, 1966

169. If literary theft be, like imitation, a sincere form of flattery, *The Colloquies of Erasmus* occupy the proud position of one of the most pillaged works in existence.
—PRESERVED SMITH, *A Key to the Colloquies of Erasmus*, 1927

170. Some time ago I asked a young gentleman . . . whether he had read a certain book. . . . "Not yet," he answered, "I like people so much better than books."
"So do I," I replied, "and that is why I like some books so much better than I like some people."
—J. DUNCAN SPAETH, Barnwell Address, May 8, 1929

171. All you can read, will be of little use, if you do not think and reason upon yourself. One reads to know other people's thoughts.
—PHILIP STANHOPE, letter, 1740

172. Buy good books, and read them; the best books are the commonest, and the last editions are always the best, if the editors are not blockheads.
— PHILIP STANHOPE, letter, March 19, 1750

173. The sleep of novels as they are read is soundless.
— MARK STRAND, "The Sleep," *Poems by Mark Strand*, 1970

174. We are so accustomed to reading novels with our minds asleep.
— G. W. STONIER, "Words! Words!" in *Gog Magog*, 1933

175. Nearly everybody in a mystery novel is a consummate athlete.
— SIMON STRUNSKY, *Sinbad and His Friends*, 1921

176. The daily book column, indeed, is a recent and more-or-less hopeless invention.
— RALPH THOMPSON, "The Popular Review and the Scholarly Book," in *English Institute Annual*, 1940

177. Let not the authority of the author be in thy way, whether he be of little or great learning; but let love of simple truth lead thee to read.
— THOMAS À KEMPIS, *The Following of Christ*, V, 1, 1425

178. Many books are no more than one-shot magazines.
— ALVIN TOFFLER, *Future Shock*, 1970

179. The incredible expansion of knowledge implies that each book (alas, this book included) contains a progressively smaller fraction of all that is known.
— ALVIN TOFFLER, *Future Shock*, 1970

180. The book (Bouvard and Pécuchet) was to him more than a work of art; it was a deed.
— LIONEL TRILLING, on Flaubert in *The Opposing Self*, 1955

181. Books are cheap; so cheap that it is hard to imagine how authors make a living.
— REBECCA WEST, *Ending in Earnest*, 1931

182. I write the sort of books which people assume to be the work of a cheerful, if backward, young fellow of twenty-five.
— P. G. WODEHOUSE, *America, I Like You*, 1956

183. To this day, I become distressed if I am anywhere without a book.

—CHARLES VAN DOREN, *The Joy of Reading*, 1985

184. I am predisposed to like the novel dealing with history and find it hard to understand why this valuable genre should be so much disdained.

—GORE VIDAL, *New York Review of Books*, May 1973

185. Despite the enormous quantity of books, how few people read!

—VOLTAIRE, "Books," *Philosophical Dictionary*, 1764

186. Today people complain of a surfeit of books. But it is not for readers to complain. The remedy is easy; nothing forces anyone to read.

—VOLTAIRE, "Books," *Philosophical Dictionary*, 1764

187. Whatever Conrad's books are or are not, it may safely be said that they are never jolly.

—HUGH WALPOLE, *Joseph Conrad*, 1916

188. No one will write books once they reach heaven, but there is an excellent library, containing all the books written up to date, including all the lost books and the ones that the authors burned when they came back from the last publisher.

—EVELYN WAUGH, *Daily Chronicle*, March 18, 1930

189. I set out to write novels, as distinguished from those pseudo-scientific stories in which imaginative experience rather than personal conduct was the matter in hand, on the assumption that problems of adjustment were the essential matter for novel writing . . . [Henry James] had no idea of the possible use of the novel as a help to conduct. His mind had turned away from any such idea. From his point of view there were not so much "novels" as THE NOVEL and it was a very high and important achievement. He thought of it as an ART FORM and novelists as artists of a very special and exalted type. . . . If THE NOVEL was properly a presentation of real people as real people, in absolutely natural reaction in a story, then my characters were not simply sketch, they were eked out by wires and pads of non-living matter and they stood condemned.

—H. G. WELLS, *Experiment in Autobiography*, 1934

190. Books, I fancy, may be conveniently divided into three classes:
1. Books to read. . . .

2. Books to reread. . . .
3. Books not to read at all. . . .
The third class is by far the most important. To tell people what to read is, as a rule, either useless or harmful; for, the appreciation of literature is a question of temperament not of teaching; to Parnassus there is no primer and nothing that one can learn is ever worth learning. But to tell people what not to read is a very different matter, and I venture to recommend it. . . . Indeed, it is one that is eminently needed in this age of ours, an age that reads so much, that it has no time to admire, and writes so much, that it has no time to think. Whoever will select out of the chaos of our modern curricula "The Worst Hundred Books" and publish a list of them, will confer on the rising generation a real and lasting benefit.

    —Oscar Wilde, *Pall Mall Gazette*, February 8, 1886

191. A novel is what one person tells us took place. . . . A novel is what one mind, claiming omniscience asserts to have existed.

    —Thornton Wilder, "Some Thoughts on Playwrighting" in *The Intent of the Artist*, 1941

192. His book lives in its second reading . . . you must know the middle of the book to know the beginning of the book.

    —Thornton Wilder, on Kafka's "The Castle," *Journal*, September 24, 1948

193. Can there be anything more ridiculous than to know what book is wanted, to have the money ready for it and not be able to find it—while it is lying on the shelf of some publisher, unsold?

    —William Carlos Williams, *The Neglected Artist*, 1936

194. A true book collector knows whether he is one or not, just as the old saying has it about being in love.

    —Robert A. Wilson, *Modern Book Collecting*, 1980

195. It is obvious that a mediocre book is always too long, and that a great one usually seems too short.

    —Edith Wharton, *The Writing of Fiction*, 1925

196. He knew not that a palace hated knowledge
And deem'd it pedantry to spell and write
Tom heard of Royal libraries indeed,
And weakly fancied that books were read.

    —John Wolcott, "To Authors, Advice to the Future Laureat," *The Works of Peter Pindar*, 1812

197. The only advice, indeed, that one person can give another about reading is to take no advice.... After all what laws can be laid down about books?
—VIRGINIA WOOLF, *The Second Common Reader*, 1932

198. Old travel books occupy so many shelves in my apartment that a visitor might take me to be some kind of antiquarian nut. I am merely a travel nut.
—WILLIAM ZINSSER, *New York Times Book Review*, August 26, 1990

199. A dictionary is the reference book that we use when we wish to ascertain the various meanings of a particular word.... Where did the meaning or meanings acquired by that meaningless notation come from to turn it into a word? ... For a [person] to get to the point at which he can move effectively within the circle of a dictionary, some meaningless notations must have become meaningful words for him — and became so without the help of a dictionary.... A meaningful word, a notation with significance, is a sign. A sign functions by presenting to the mind for its attention an object other than itself.
—MORTIMER J. ADLER, *Ten Philosophical Mistakes*, 1985

200. What to admire ... what to hope ... what to love ... and how would I meet them myself? Simply by never, so far as I could help it, letting a child read what is not worth reading.
—JOHN RUSKIN, "Fors Clavigera," Letter 50, *Agnes' Book*, 1885–1889

201. No days, perhaps, of all our childhood are ever so fully lived as those that we had regarded as not being lived at all: days spent wholly with a favorite book.
—MARCEL PROUST, "Day of Reading 1" from
Introduction to *Sesame and Lilies*, 1906

202. The old novel which we used to read, and to which the world so fondly clings, had no idea of relation or perspective.
—CLARENCE DARROW, *Realism in Literature*, 1899

203. I would be most content if my children grew up to be the kind of people who think decorating consists mostly of building enough bookshelves.
—ANNA QUINDLEN, "Enough Bookshelves,"
New York Times, August 7, 1991

204. Reading has always been life unwrapped to me, a way of understanding the world and understanding myself through both the unknown and the everyday.

—ANNA QUINDLEN, "Enough Bookshelves,"
New York Times, August 7, 1991

205. There were four books in our house when I was growing up, and reading for pleasure was not approved of. It was thought to be dangerous, like pure laughter.

—JOHN MCGAHERN, "Me Among the Protestants,"
New York Times Book Review, April 28, 1991

• Journalism/Press •

206. I am unable to comprehend how a man of honour could take a newspaper in his hands without a shudder of disgust.

—CHARLES BAUDELAIRE, *Intimate Journals*, 1857

207. I have always secretly admired people who could read a newspaper while eating.

—ROBERT BENCHLEY, *My Ten Years in a Quandary*, 1936

208. A newspaper dies with the day, and its contents in general die with it.

—WILLIAM COWPER, letter, May 19, 1788

209. Journalism ain't history.

—ANTHONY R. DOLAN, letter to *New York Times*,
January 13, 1991

210. All newsmen should make brief speeches, but before I begin.

—WES GALLAGHER, speech, February 10, 1967

211. If asked to name the most important institution in our lives, one would have to say the underground newspaper.

—ABBIE HOFFMAN, *Steal This Book*, 1971

212. Let's face it, the aim of a good high school newspaper should be to destroy the high school.

—ABBIE HOFFMAN, *Steal This Book*, 1971

213. A whisper may fly as quick and be as pernicious as a pamphlet.
— DAVID HUME, "Of the Liberty of the Press," 1752

214. The press is used to make the victim look like the criminal and make the criminal look like the victim.
— MALCOLM X, speech, Rochester, New York, February 16, 1965

215. American newspapers and journals (with certain notable and honorable exceptions) are not written "upwards" . . . but downwards so as to catch the ear and capture the money of the crowd.
— STEPHEN LEACOCK, *Essays and Literary Studies*, 1922

216. Fiction properly so called, or the imaginative tale, frolics across the average daily paper, enjoying the most prominent spots even to the top of the page.
— MARSHALL MCLUHAN, quoting Mallarmé in "Joyce, Mallarmé and the Press," *Sewanee Review*, Vol. 62, No. 1, Winter 1954

217. It means becoming a journalist again which I loathe and abhor.
— HAROLD NICOLSON, diary, September 14, 1933

218. It is finally getting home to me that Americans don't love the press.
— DANIEL SCHORR, speech, December 14, 1978

219. Virtually every newspaper reader survey I have seen shows that the columnists are read more than the editorials are read. The reason is . . . we have some feel for the person.
— (SENATOR) PAUL SIMON, letter to the *New York Times*, May 6, 1990

220. The best journalism is nothing but realism.
— JOHN FARRAR, *The Literary Spotlight*, 1924

• Language •

221. Words represent things and (the poets) had also the human voice at their disposal, which of all our organs can best represent other things. . . . Language to be good must be clear, as is proved by the fact that speech which fails to convey a plain message will fail to do just what speech has to do. . . . Even in poetry it is not quite appropriate that fine language should be used by . . . a very young man, or about trivial subjects. . . . All the more so in prose, where the subject-matter is less exalted. We can now see that a writer must disguise his art and give the impression of speaking naturally and not artificially. Naturalness is persuasive, artificiality is the contrary.

—ARISTOTLE, *Rhetoric*, Book III

222. It is difficult at the present time to determine how large the debt of English is to the American vocabulary.

—ALBERT BAUGH, *A History of the English Language*, 1935

223. Language, *n*. The music with which we charm the serpents guarding another's treasures.

—AMBROSE BIERCE, *The Devil's Dictionary*, 1911

224. It is not possible for language to be totally precise; if we attempt to make a scientific system both finite and complete, it turns out to contain irremovable paradoxes.

—JACOB BRONOWSKI, *A Sense of the Future*, 1977

225. The English language is ruled by two despots . . . the names of these two stout rulers are Use and Custom, and their authority extends over every province of the English language.

—JOHN BUNKER "Two English Despots," in
The College Book of Essays, 1939

226. I have become more doubtful about language as a necessary paradigm for thinking. If we think in terms of music, is that a language?

—FRITJOB CAPRA, quoting R. D. Laing in
Uncommon Wisdom, 1986

227. Writers search their memories for a better word to use in a given context but are no more in the habit of questioning language than of questioning the weather.

—STUART CHASE, *The Tyranny of Words*, 1938

228. If I had not written in English I would not have written at all.

—JOSEPH CONRAD, *A Personal Record*, 2nd Preface, 1919

229. So long as the English tongue survives, the word Dunderque [sic] will be spoken with reverence.

—ROBERT L. DUFFUS, *New York Times*, June 1, 1940

230. If language is to lead at all to understanding, there must be rules.
— ALBERT EINSTEIN, *The Common Language of Science*, 1941

231. English is a language ill suited to good prose because of the associations that, like burrs, cling undetachable to every English word.
— FORD MADDOX FORD, letter to
Saturday Review of Literature, May 1939

232. Language, like love, starts local.
— ALLAN GURGANUS, "A Hog Loves Its Life,"
The Quarterly, No. 11, Fall 1989

233. Chimp language has been a controversial area for over a decade now. While it appears that these and other primates can absorb numerous vocabulary items — up to several hundred, in fact, — and even on occasion come up with ingenious compound words, it is far less well substantiated that they can absorb a grammar by which they can combine words into complex meaning-carrying propositions. It seems that chimps may simply use arbitrary juxtapositions of words rather than syntactic structures. Is this a severe limitation? In the eyes of some it is, for it puts a strict upper bound to the complexity of ideas that can be expressed thereby. Noam Chomsky and others maintain that that which is essentially human is our innate language ability, a sort of "primal grammar" that all languages would share at a sufficiently deep level. Thus chimps and other primates not sharing our primal grammar would be essentially different from us. . . . Rather than communicating — that is, converting private ideas into the common currency of signs in patterns — they [chimps] are manipulating symbols that to them have no meaning, but whose manipulation can achieve desired goals for them.
— DOUGLAS R. HOFSTADTER, *The Mind's I*, 1981

234. The slangy, idiomatic, frequently vulgar language which Twain and Salinger put in the mouths of their heros is remarkable for the clarity of the self-portraits that emerge, as well as for the effortless accuracy of the talk itself.
— CHARLES KAPLAN, "Holden and Huck: The Odysseys of Youth," in *College English*, XVIII, November 1956

235. The language is like a great organ, and the various classes of words are like its stops. The more stops, that is, the greater the number of kinds of words, the more varied and the richer are the effects which

can be produced by the artist who is capable of playing upon the language.
— GEORGE PHILIP KRAPP, "Profit and Loss
in Word-Borrowing," *Modern English*, 1909

236. [Many examples indicate] the unconscious use of sensuous metaphor by which language expands as expansion is needed. Apparently the words which lend themselves most readily to metaphysical uses are those which denote light, heat, movement, or faintness, dullness, also pain and threat . . . . All these words either have direct application to mental states and acts, or have close cognates that are obvious extensions to psychical phenomena. It appears that light, smoothness and especially movement are the natural symbols of life, freedom and joy, as darkness and immobility, roughness and hardness are the symbols of death and frustration.
— SUSANNE LANGER, *Mind: An Essay on Human Feeling*, Vol. I, 1967

237. It is at once obvious that the question, "What is language?" is a highly peculiar one. It is so because, in order to ask the question, we have to make use of the very language about which we are asking.
— JOHN MACQUARRIE, *God-Talk*, 1967

238. When it comes to deciding what is not good English, there are almost as many points of view as there are persons to hold them.
— ALBERT MARCHWARDT, "What Is Good English,"
in *Essays Old and New*, 1940

239. No one understands the constriction of a sentence who does not understand punctuation. That statement is undebatable, and its corollary, that no one understands his own thought who does not also understand the construction of his sentence, is equally undebatable.
— PERCY MARKS, "Punctuation" from *The Craft of Writing*, 1932

240. The only function of language, as I see it, is the direct expression of the thought.
— DON MARQUIS, letter to Josephine Piercy, March 27, 1925

241. In terms of the extensions of man, the theme of the dragon's teeth in the Cadmus myth is of the utmost importance. Elias Canetti in *Crowds and Power* reminds us that the teeth are an obvious agent of power in man, and especially in many animals. Languages are filled with testimony to the grasping devouring power and precision of teeth. That the power of letters as agents of aggressive order and precision should be expressed as extensions of the dragon's teeth is natural and fitting. Teeth are emphatically visual in their lineal order. Letters are not only like teeth visually, but their power to put teeth into the business of empire-building is manifest in our Western history.... It can be argued, then, that the phonetic alphabet, alone, is the technology that has been the means of creating "civilized man"—the separate individuals equal before a written code of law.

—MARSHALL MCLUHAN, *Understanding Media: The Extensions of Man*, 1964

242. I guess our ancient speech has gone so flat that we have to spike it.

—OGDEN NASH, *You Can't Get There from Here*, 1957

243. I am not good at languages, and grammar has had no attraction for me whatever.

—JAWAHARLAL NEHRU, *Toward Freedom*, 1941

244. Look at the question of the use of "vulgar, vile, or filthy words...." We are weakening the lusty English language by rejecting them.

—SEAN O'CASEY, *Blasts and Benedictions*, 1950

245. Today, realism has become one of the most silly, beastly and degraded words in the language.

—SEAN O'FAOLIAN, *A Summer in Italy*, 1948

246. Writers are the servants of the language. Language is the common property of society, and writers are the guardians of language.

—OCTAVIO PAZ, on being awarded the Nobel Prize, *The New York Times*, October 12, 1990

247. We seldom miss language, because it is so readily available.

—MARIO PEI, *One Language for the World*, 1961

248. Language is based on reason, antiquity, authority and usage.

—QUINTILIAN, Book I, vi, 1

249. The writer must create his own language, and not use that of his neighbors. He must be able to watch it grow.

—JULES RENARD, *Journal*, June 1902

250. He did not speak to them without a parable.

—GOSPEL OF ST. MARK, 4:34

251. English is a stretch language: one size fits all. That does not mean anything goes; in most instances anything does not go.
—WILLIAM SAFIRE, *On Language*, 1980

252. There are no handles upon a language whereby men take hold of it.
—CARL SANDBURG, *Chicago Poems*, 1916

253. The main effect of language consists in its meaning, in the ideas which it expresses. But no expression is possible without a presentation, and this presentation must have a form.... No word has the exact value of any other in the same or in another language. But the intrinsic effect of language does not stop there. The single word is but a stage in the series of formations which constitute language, and which preserve for me the fruit of their experience, distilled and concentrated into a symbol.... Grammar, philosophically studied, is akin to the deepest metaphysics, because in revealing the constitution of speech, it reveals the constitution of thought, and the hierarchy of those categories by which we conceive the world. It is by virtue of this ... development that language has its function of expressing experience with exactness, and the poet—to whom language is an instrument of art—has to employ it also with a constant reference to meaning and veracity; that is, he must be a master of experience before he can become a true master of words.
—GEORGE SANTAYANA, *The Sense of Beauty*, 1896

254. With the possible exception of a baseball umpire or a movie critic, there is no more popular object of abuse than the English language.
—JOHN SIMON, *Paradigms Lost*, 1979

255. Language is the most impure, the most contaminated, the most exhausted of all the materials out of which art is made.
—SUSAN SONTAG, *Styles of Radical Will*, 1969

256. Language grows and evolves, leaving fossils behind. The individual words are like different species of animals. Mutations occur. Words fuse, and then mate.
—LEWIS THOMAS, *A Long Line of Cells: Collected Essays*, 1990

257. A perfectly healthy sentence, it is true, is extremely rare.
—HENRY DAVID THOREAU, "On Style in Writing" in
A Week on the Concord and Merrimack Rivers, 1848

258. Without language, there is no way to understand the passage of time.
　　　　—LOU ANN WALKER, *New York Times*, February 3, 1991

259. Mankind likes to have its wisdom presented in potted form. Every civilized language is rich in proverbs.
　　　　—ERNEST WECKLEY, *Something About Words*, 1935

260. The instrument for censorship of the subversive works not only on literature but on language.
　　　　—REBECCA WEST, *Ending in Earnest*, 1931

261. I enjoy etymology; it is a fascinating game. If one is a student of the evolution of language, it is something a good deal more than a game.
　　　　—STEPHEN WHITE, Afterword in *The New Liberal Arts*
　　　　An Alfred P. Sloan Foundation Paper, August 1981

262. As advertising blather becomes the nation's normal idiom, language becomes printed noise.
　　　　—GEORGE WILL, *The Pursuit of Happiness*, 1978

263. The humorist [Mr. Dooley] said that when Americans were finished with the English language it would look as if it had been run over by a musical comedy.
　　　　—GEORGE WILL, *The Pursuit of Happiness*, 1978

264. Only in a few cases and in a few kinds of literature have writers been able to make a living.
　　　　—RUPERT BROOKE, "Democracy and the Arts,"
　　　　Paper to Cambridge University Fabian Society, 1910

265. A writer can create and develop a character through her or his use of language. An upper-class person will draw from a more Latinate word pool and use more subordinate clauses and longer, less volatile speech rhythms. A character from the lower classes will use more Anglo-Saxon words, much more colorful speech patterns and shorter, staccato rhythms unless this character is from the American South. In that case, rich and poor alike are more prone to use the rhythm of the King James version of the Bible. Here again, the poor characters will employ more Anglo-Saxon words and will probably be more emotionally direct.
　　　　—RITA MAE BROWN, "To the Victor Belongs the Language,"
　　　　in *New York Times Book Review*, December 20, 1987

266. For the poet, language is a structure of the external world. The speaker is in a situation in language; he is invested by words. They are prolongations of his senses, his pincers, his antennae, his spectacles. He manoeuvres them from within; he feels them as if they were his body; he is surrounded by a verbal body which he is hardly conscious of and which extends his action upon the world. The poet is outside language. He sees the reverse side of words, as if he did not share the human condition and as if he were first meeting the work as a barrier as he comes towards men. Instead of first knowing things by their name, it seems that first he has a silent contact with them, since, turning towards the other species of thing which for him is the word, touching words, testing them, fingering them, he discovers in them a slight luminosity of their own and particular affinities with the earth, the sky, the water, and all created things.

—JEAN-PAUL SARTRE, *What Is Literature? and Other Essays*, 1965

267. Organize
The Language
Right.

WILLIAM CARLOS WILLIAMS, from "Africa" in
The Collected Earlier Poems, 1951

268. We use language so badly that we become the slaves of our clichés and are turned either into conforming Babbitts or into fanatics and doctrinaires . . . which merely confirms what every writer painfully discovers for himself—that full communication with a large audience is impossible, that most people read into literature the standardized notions with which they set out, that the author's laborious efforts to find an adequate verbal equivalent for experience are simply not noticed by the majority of his readers, who automatically transform what Mallarmé calls the *sens plus* of the artist's language into the soiled and shopworn *mots de la tribu*. Language, it is evident, has its own Gresham's Law. Bad words tend to drive out good words, and words in general, the good as well as the bad, tend to drive out immediate experience and our memories of immediate experience. And yet without words there would be precious little memory of any kind.

—ALDOUS HUXLEY, *Tomorrow and Tomorrow and Tomorrow*, 1964

• Literature •

269. For fiction, read Scott alone; all novels after his are worthless.

—CHARLOTTE BRONTË, letter to Ellen Nussey, July 4, 1834

270. Every type of literature, regardless of its length or brevity of duration, or instance of appearance, has its original and motivating cause in environment.
— V. F. CALVERTON, *The Newer Spirit*, 1925

271. If there is anything worth criticizing in contemporary American literature it is our fiction.
— HENRY SEIDAL CANBY, *Definitions*, 1922

272. Literature will neither yield thee bread, nor a stomach to digest bread with; quit it in God's name.
— THOMAS CARLYLE, letter to Ralph Waldo Emerson, February 3, 1835

273. Language and myth are near of kin.
— ERNST CASSIRER, *An Essay on Man*, 1944

274. Any man who undertakes to talk about history as literature ought to begin by expressing his deep conviction that when it becomes literature history does not in any way cease to be history.
— BRUCE CATTON, *Prefaces to History*, 1970

275. The poet appears as a magician who gives to things a language in which they proclaim their own being, but they come alive only in the soul of the poet, only in an inner world.
— RUDOLF EUCKEN, Nobel Lecture, March 27, 1909

276. My first book was published in 1949 and at that time I knew nothing of [politics]; I was filled with literature, that's all.
— NADINE GORDIMER, *New York Times*, January 1, 1991

277. Fantasy, like the marketing genres before it, has been made predictable, has eliminated new ideas and can now be sold as product.
— DAVID G. HARTWELL, "Dollars and Dragons," in *The New York Times Book Review*, April 29, 1990

278. I did not connect the grown men and women in literature with the grown men and women I saw around me. They were, to me, another species.
— LILLIAN HELLMAN, *An Unfinished Woman*, 1969

279. "Politics in a work of literature," wrote Stendhal, "is like a pistol-shot in the middle of a concert, something loud and vulgar, and

yet a thing to which it is not possible to refuse one's attention."
—IRVING HOWE, quoting Stendhal in *Politics and the Novel*, 1957

280. Literature need not be dust just because we fleshpeople return to it.
—ERICA JONG, *At the Edge of the Body*, 1979

281. Hamlet is a great play, written from the standpoint of a ghost.
—JAMES JOYCE, attributed to Djuna Barnes
in *Interviews*, April 1922

282. Charity, of course, is what the writer supports himself with while he is finishing his novel. Hope is the virtue by which he firmly trusts that someday, somewhere, somebody will publish his novel. But it is in the virtue of faith that the writer grounds himself or herself in the true religious experience of literature.
—WILLIAM KENNEDY, "Why It Took So Long,"
New York Times Book Review, May 20, 1990

283. You can't really write a romance now, it has been ceded to the bargain-basement depths of literature.
—PAUL MONETTE, interview in
New York Times Book Review, March 4, 1990

284. A great value of antiquity lies in the fact that its writings are the only ones that modern men still read with exactness.
—FRIEDRICH NIETZSCHE, Notes, 1874

285. Literature is the last great cottage industry. Every person or novel is a one-of-a-kind thing, made at home, by hand.
—JAY PARINI, "The More They Write, the More
They Write," *New York Times*, July 30, 1989

286. The chief material of literature is human nature, which never changes; poets, dramatists, novelists, satirists focus their attention on man's thoughts, and loves and hates.
—WILLIAM LYON PHELPS, *The Advance of the English Novel*, 1927

287. Literature is language charged with meaning.
—EZRA POUND, *ABC of Reading*, 1934

288. Great literature is simply language charged with meaning to the utmost possible degree.
—EZRA POUND, *ABC of Reading*, 1934

289. Literature is news that STAYS news.
— EZRA POUND, *ABC of Reading*, 1934

290. The true nature of poetry. The drive to connect. The dream of a common language.
— ADRIENNE RICH, *The Dream of a Common Language*, 1978

291. It was an old theme even for me: language cannot do everything.
— ADRIENNE RICH, *The Dream of a Common Language*, 1978

292. To turn events into ideas is the function of literature.
— GEORGE SANTAYANA, "The Essence of Literature," in *The Life of Reason*, 1905

293. Homer remains, translations come and go. Only the very best, like Pope's survive their own age as literature in their own right.
— OLIVER TAPLIN, *New York Times Book Review*, October 7, 1990

294. One is sometimes tempted to think that the generation which has invented the "fiction course" is getting the fiction it deserves.
— EDITH WHARTON, *The Writing of Fiction*, 1925

• Poets and Poetry •

295. When a critic sneers at the public taste, as critics often do, it proves only that he is very well satisfied with his own; when a poet does so, as poets commonly do, it proves no more than that he is not popular, and considers he ought to be. In every age poets complain that they have no public; in every age, on the other hand, the public complain that they have no poets.
— A. ST. JOHN. ADCOCK, *Modern Grub Street*, 1913

296. I think of course that no attempt should be made to express in the form of a poem what could possibly be expressed in prose. Am I right in this?
— SHERWOOD ANDERSON, letter to Carl Sandburg, April 1917

297. What poets feel not, when they make,
A pleasure in creating,

The world, in it turn, will not take
Pleasure in contemplating.
— MATTHEW ARNOLD, *A Caution to Poets*, 1867

298. It is a sad fact about our culture that a poet can earn much more money writing or talking about his art then he can by practicing it. All the poems I have written were written for love; naturally, when I have written one, I try to market it, but the prospect of a market played no role in its writing.
— W. H. AUDEN, Foreword, *The Dyer's Hand*, 1962

299. Critics are inclined to think, and have always been inclined to think, that if a poet is popular he must be bad.
— MAURICE BARING, *Lost Lectures*, 1932

300. "Many a gem" the poet mourns, abides forgotten in the dust, unnoticed there.
— CHARLES BAUDELAIRE, "Artist Unknown,"
from *Les Fleurs du Mal*, 1857

301. Always be a poet, even in prose.
— CHARLES BAUDELAIRE, "My Heart Laid Bare,"
in *Intimate Journals*, 1864

302. Where is the sense of reading poetry or fiction unless you see more beauty, more passion, more scope for your sympathy, than you saw before?
— ARNOLD BENNETT, *Things That Have Interested Me*, 1921

303. Your poems tease me to the verge of tears.
— JOHN BERRYMAN, note to Wang Wei
from *His Thoughts Made Pockets*, 1958

304. Imagination, *n.* A warehouse of facts, with poet and liar in joint ownership.
— AMBROSE BIERCE, *The Devil's Dictionary*, 1911

305. Poets prefer to dwell in solitude.
— BOCCACCIO, *Genealogy of the Gods*, XIV, 1363

306. The way to develop good taste in literature is to read poetry. If you think that I am speaking out of professional partisanship, that I am trying to advance my own guild interests, you are badly mistaken.

For, being the supreme form of human locution, poetry is not only the most concise, the most condensed way of conveying the human experience; it also offers the highest possible standards for any linguistic operation—especially one on paper. The more one reads poetry, the less tolerant one becomes of any sort of verbosity, be that in political or philosophical discourse, be that in history, social studies or the art of fiction. Good style in prose is always hostage to the precision, speed and laconic intensity of poetic diction. A child of epitaph and epigram, conceived indeed as a short cut to any conceivable subject matter, poetry to prose is a great disciplinarian. It teaches the latter not only the value of each word but also the mercurial mental patterns of the species, alternatives to linear composition, the knack of omitting the self-evident, emphasis on detail, the technique of anticlimax. Above all poetry develops in prose that appetite for metaphysics that distinguishes a work of art from mere belle-lettres.
—JOSEPH BRODSKY, "How to Read a Book," Speech at the Book Fair, Turin, Italy, May 18, printed in *The New York Times*, July 12, 1988

307. Randall Jarrell was the best poetry critic of his time, but of course he wanted to be the best poet.
—ANATOLE BROYARD, *New York Times Book Review*, May 6, 1990

308. Poetry is the worst mask in the world behind which folly and stupidity could attempt to hide their features.
—WILLIAM CULLEN BRYANT, Lectures on Poetry, April 1825

309. It is part of my creed that the only poetry is history, could we tell it right.
—THOMAS CARLYLE, letter to Ralph Waldo Emerson, August 12, 1834

310. His perpetual never-failing tendency to transform into shape, into life, the opinion, the feeling that may dwell in him; which, in its widest sense, we reckon to be essentially the grand problem of the poet.
—THOMAS CARLYLE, essay, "Goethe," 1828

311. All poets have to be critics, and they can fitly be called great critics when the theories they evolve about their own work influence others.
—MARY M. COLUM, *From These Roots*, 1937

312. I must allow that the effect of poetry should be to lift the mind from the painful realities of actual existence.
—GEORGE CRABBE, Preface to *The Tales*, 1812

313. The poet owns thy powers
Hope leads him on, and every fear devours
He writes, and unsuccessful, writes again.
—GEORGE CRABBE, "Hope," *Wheble's Magazine*, 1772

314. A prose writer gets tired of writing prose, and wants to be a poet. So he begins every line with a capital letter, and keeps on writing prose.
—SAMUEL MCCHORD CROTHERS, "Every Man's Natural Desire to Be Somebody Else" from *The Dame School of Experience*, 1920

315. Rash author, 't is a vain presumptuous crime
To undertake the sacred art of rhyme
If at thy birth the stars that rul'd thy sense
Shone not with a poetic influence.
—BOILEAU, *The Art of Poetry*, 1683

316. Poetry has a universal language which tells of the universal experiences of all time, but prose has not.
—ELIZABETH DREW, *The Modern Novel*, 1926

317. What every poet starts from is his own emotions. And when we get down to these, there is not much to choose between Shakespeare and Dante.... The great poet, in writing himself, writes his time. Thus Dante, hardly knowing it, became the voice of the thirteenth century; Shakespeare, hardly knowing it, became the representative of the end of the sixteenth century, of a turning point in history.... If Shakespeare had written according to a better philosophy, he would have written worse poetry; it was his business to express the greatest emotional intensity of his time, based on whatever his time happened to think. Poetry is not a substitute for philosophy or theology or religion ... it has its own function. But as this function is not intellectual but emotional, it cannot be defined adequately in intellectual terms.
—T. S. ELIOT, essay, "Shakespeare and the Stoicism of Seneca," 1927

318. I alone of English writers have consciously set myself to make music out of what I may call the sound of sense. Now it is possible to have sense without the sound of sense (as in much prose that is supposed to pass muster but makes very dull reading) and the sound of sense without sense (as in *Alice in Wonderland* which makes anything but dull reading). The best place to get the abstract sound of sense is from voices behind a door that cuts off the words ... the sound of sense then ... it is the abstract vitality of our speech. It is pure sound—pure

form. One who concerns himself with it more than the subject is an artist.
— ROBERT FROST, letter to John T. Bartlett, July 3, 1913

319. I love it that the Celtic god of poetry is a pig.
— JOHN GARDNER, "John Napper Sailing Through the Universe" in *The King's Indian*, 1972

320. Poetry is a sacred incarnation of a smile. Poetry is a sigh that dries the tears.
— KAHLIL GIBRAN, "Poets and Poems" in *Thoughts and Meditations*, 1960

321. The drama editor had noticed that Gene chewed tobacco while writing poetry, and that such a sight should be preserved.
— LAWRENCE GREEN about Gene Fowler, in *Esquire*, February 1953

322. I quite early came to understand that poetry was a matter of what I will call interior stance. A man was either swept into that stance or willed himself into it.
— WILLIAM GOLDING, "My First Book" from *The Author*, July 1981

323. I pray that with my lot I may be satisfied;
My mind and vigor stay.
— HORACE, Ode I, 31

324. My two years in Washington were unhappy years, except for poetry and the friends I made through poetry. I wrote many poems. I always put them away new for several weeks in a bottom drawer. Then I would take them out and re-read them. If they seemed bad, I would throw them away. They would all seem good when I wrote them and, usually, bad when I would look at them again. So most of them were thrown away.
— LANGSTON HUGHES, *The Big Sea*, 1940

325. A poet must at the same time, and necessarily, be a historian and a philosopher.
— VICTOR HUGO, *William Shakespeare*, Book I, Part II, Chapter 1, 1864

326. A poet; for all writers he has the best chance for immortality. Others may write from the head, but he writes from the heart, and the heart will always understand him.
— WASHINGTON IRVING, "The Mutability of Literature," *The Sketch Book of Geoffrey Crayon, Gent.*, 1820

327. Philosophers are after all like poets. They are path-finders. What everyone can feel, what everyone can know in the bone and marrow of him, they sometimes can find words for and express. The words and thoughts of the philosophers are not exactly the words and thoughts of the poets — worse luck. But both alike have the same function. They are, if I may use a simile, so many spots, or blazes, — blazes made by the axe of the human intellect on the trees of the otherwise trackless forest of human experience. They give you somewhere to go from. They give us a direction and a place to reach. . . . The blazes give a sort of ownership. We can now use the forest, wind across it with companions, and enjoy its quality. It is no longer a place merely to get lost in and never return.

— WILLIAM JAMES, *Pragmatism*, 1907

328. A poem doesn't exist till it's written.
— RANDALL JARRELL, letter to Edmund Wilson, January 1941

329. I write poetry to investigate myself, and my meaning and meanings.
— LEROI JONES, "Gatsby's Theory of Aesthetics,"
in *Sabotage*, 1961–1963

330. You may look for the same themes from the greatest poet and the least.
— JUVENAL, "Satires," I

331. Not of his own will the Poet
sings. There is a spark that sometimes kindles,
and when it kindles inflames
and when it inflames possesses
and embraces the Poet, as if, kissing him
telling him words that none but he understands.
— DUN KARM, from "Shadow and Light" in *Dell U Dija*, June 1932

332. Poets are followed by none save erring men. Behold how aimlessly they rove in every valley preaching what they never practice.
— THE KORAN, The Poets, Chapter 26, verse 24–25

333. A line which rings true is usually the embryo of a poem. But how that line arose in the poet's mind cannot be generally described.
— SUSANNE LANGER, *Mind: An Essay on Human Feeling*, 1967

334. "Did you know that [an unidentified poet friend] was writing his autobiography?"

"I did."

"Why, why didn't you stop him?"

"How would I stop him?"

"You know perfectly well, Cecil, that no poet should ever write an autobiography."

"Oh."

"Has he got it here [in Venice]?"

"Probably."

"Then we'll go and burn it."

The project—I mean the burning—was fortunately abandoned.

— C. DAY LEWIS, *The Buried Day—A Conversation with Auden*, 1960

335. The poem, clearly, is like a score and the readings like performances. Different renderings are admissible. The question is not which is the "right" one but which is the best.

— C. S. LEWIS, *An Experiment in Criticism*, 1965

336. When a great poet has said a thing, it is finally and utterly expressed, and has as many meanings as there are men who read his verse.

— JAMES RUSSELL LOWELL, *The Function of the Poet and Other Essays*, 1920

337. The poet, under whatever name, always stands for the same thing—imagination.

— JAMES RUSSELL LOWELL, "The Function of the Poet," *Century Magazine*, January 1894

338. Poets in particular find it hard to look at plays with serenity. No two arts are more opposed than our poetry and our theater. In comparison with poetry, theater, even Off-Broadway and even in its losses, is a highly popular medium. Even though the playwright faces much greater difficulty in making the grade than other writers, and even though he is nothing if he fails, yet if he succeeds, the uproar of praise is unbelievable. His hits are almost national events. Yet the literary prestige of our plays is wobbly. Even the great, even O'Neill, even Williams, seem more on the fringe of our high cultures than part of it. They are seen rather than read, and are very grudgingly allowed to be writers.

At the other extreme are our poets. They are little read, cause no sensations, and live on grants. Yet, if publication is achieved, though sales are non-existent, the prizes are many, and poets enjoy a quiet, unquestioned, firm renown. Our poetry may not even be considered American, or even involved with the human race, but at least what poets write is literature.

— ROBERT LOWELL, *Poets and the Theater*, 1963

339. As a matter of fact, if we know the existence of this inaudible music, within the soul of the poet, it is because in listening to the poem — especially to "modern" or post–Baudelaire poems — a similar music is awakened within our own soul ... I am obliged to speak of the poet before speaking of the poem and of the one who listens to it. Furthermore, I am confronted with a special difficulty, because I am dealing with something I must look for behind the words, as if I were in the presence of the emotional movements within the imagination of the poet, before the production of the words.

Here then, we have, I think, a first stage, merely imaginal and emotional, in the expression of poetic experience. It is transient and tendential, it tends to verbal expression, and as a matter of fact it may now and then take place at the same time as the outpouring of words and their "arrangement on paper" ... which is the second and final stage.

— JACQUES MARITAIN, *Creative Intuition in Art and Poetry*, 1953

340. Some of the epigrams are good,
Some mediocre, some bad.
Otherwise, it is understood
A Bookful of Poems cannot be had.
— MARTIAL, *Epigrams*, i, 16, circa 80 A.D.

341. To have nothing is poetry.
— EDWIN MORGAN, *Opening the Cage*, 1968

342. Poets lie, said Plato; but novelists don't always tell the truth either.
— MARVIN MUDRICK, "Fiction and Truth," *Hudson Review*, Spring 1972

343. A good couplet will outlast a bad epic.
— PHILIP MURRAY, *Poems After Martial*, 1967

344. Show me an optimist and, almost without exception, I'll show you a bad poet.
— G. J. NATHAN, *Monks Are Monks*, 1929

345. Poets, insofar as they wish to ease men's lives, either avert their glance from the arduous present, or else help the present acquire new colors by making a light shine in from the past. To be able to do this, they themselves must in some respects be creatures facing backwards, so that they can be used as bridges to quite distant times and ideas, to religions and cultures dying out or dead. . . . Of course, some unfavorable things can be said about their ways of easing life; they soothe

and heal only temporarily, only for the moment; they even prevent men from working on a true improvement of their condition, by suspending and, like a palliative, relieving the very passion of the dissatisfied who are compelled to act.
—FRIEDRICH NIETZSCHE, *Human, All Too Human*, 1878

346. Poetry is of all arts the most national, or should I rather say, local . . . whereas prose can always be adequately translated . . . poetry is almost untranslatable.
—GEORGE ORWELL, *English Poetry Since 1900*, June 13, 1943

347. O mortals
Dumb in cold fear of death, why do you trouble
St. Stygian rivers, shadows, empty names
The lying stock of poets.
—OVID, *Metamorphoses*, Book XV, lines 156–159

348. The poet is not an alchemist
The poet is a man like everyone else
A bricklayer who builds his wall:
A builder of doors and windows.
—NICANOR PARRA, *Manifesto*, 1964

349. A number of writers of my age as well as myself went through the years of our youth with Blok as our guide. Blok had everything that goes to make a great poet: fire, tenderness, emotion, his own image of the world, his own special gift for transforming everything he touched . . . his roving intentness, the rapidity of his observations . . . adjective without nouns, predicates without subjects, hide-and-seek breathless agitation, nimbly darting little figures, abruptness—how the style seemed to agree with the spirit of the age, hiding, secretive, underground, barely emerged from the cellars, talking in the language of conspirators. . . .
—BORIS PASTERNAK, *"I Remember," Sketch for an Autobiography*, 1959

350. A piece of paper contained a certain amount of information. It seemed as though the information had itself, without being asked, settled down on the sheet of printed paper, as though no one had composed and written the poem. It seemed as though the page were covered not with verses about wind and puddles, street lamps and stars, but the street lamps and puddles themselves were spreading their wind-blown ripples on the surface of the journal, as though they themselves had left the damp imprints that exerted so powerful an influence in the reader.
—BORIS PASTERNAK, *"I Remember," Sketch for an Autobiography*, 1959

351. Poetry is not identical with history, but poets who are leading the struggle know that there are no special answers.
— OCTAVIO PAZ, attributed by Pete Hamill, *Esquire*, March 1991

352. The poet who would bring uninterruptedly together such letters as t h s p and r, has either no ear at all, or two unusually long ones.
— EDGAR ALLAN POE on Algernon Henry Perkins,
Graham's Magazine, April 1842

353. A poem, in my opinion, is opposed to a work of science by having, for its immediate object, pleasure, not truth.
— EDGAR ALLAN POE, Letter to B—,
Southern Literary Messenger, July 1836

354. Poetry begins to atrophy when it gets too far from music.
— EZRA POUND, *ABC of Reading*, 1934

355. The poet's life has its small events like the lives of other men.
— MARCEL PROUST, *Poet and Novelist*, 1899

356. A really definitive study of the tricks that poetry plays with syntax would be illuminating, and delicious.
— JOHN CROWE RANSOM, "The Art and the Philosophers,"
Kenyon Review, Spring 1939

357. A poem can begin with a lie. And be torn up.
— ADRIENNE RICH, *The Dream of a Common Language*, 1978

358. To write poetry: you have to be prepared to die.
— THEODORE ROETHKE, quoted by Erica Jong
in *At the Edge of the Body*, 1979

359. Nothing is rarer than good poetry—and nothing more discouraging than the writing of poetry.
— ISAAC ROSENBERG, letter to Ruth Löry, 1912

360. (The poet) must be a master of experience before he can become a true master of words.
— GEORGE SANTAYANA, "The Sense of Beauty," in *Form in Words*, 1896

361. Baudelaire wrote his poems in order to rediscover his own image in them.
— JEAN-PAUL SARTRE, *Baudelaire*, 1950

362. Never durst poet touch a pen to write
Until his ink were tempered with love's sighs.
—SHAKESPEARE, *Love's Labour's Lost,* IV, iii.

363. Poetry is a mirror which makes beautiful that which is distorted.
—PERCY SHELLEY, *A Defence of Poetry,* 1821

364. He first begins, as Poets use,
To play his devoirs to the Muse
Then vows, if now she'll mend his pen
He'll never pester her again.
—RICHARD SHERIDAN, *Clio's Protest,* 1771

365. Poems which appear strangest to us deal with the growth of consciousness—or with consciousness awakening from sleep.
—EDITH SITWELL, letter to Allanah Harper, 1928

366. The poem of the mind in the act of finding what will suffice.
—WALLACE STEVENS, *Collected Poems,* 1964

367. Ink runs from the corners of my mouth
There is no happiness like mine.
I have been eating poetry.
—MARK STRAND, "Eating Poetry," from *Reasons for Moving,* 1968

368. We have heard much about the poetry of mathematics, but very little of it has yet been sung.
—HENRY DAVID THOREAU, *A Week on the Concord and Merrimack Rivers,* 1849

369. One of the poems I turned in was only two lines long, but it doesn't matter how long a thing is. There still has to be a beginning and an end and you have to have an idea.
—CALVIN TRILLING, *Lears,* January 1991

370. Poetry has never had its form. The origins of the ode are ancient but it was once created if not by a single ambitious schoolteacher, then by a number of poets roving like Terence's rose down the centuries. Certainly in this century poetry has gone off in as many directions as the novel, an art form whose tutelary deity is Proteus. The more like something else the novel is, the more like its true self it is. And since we do not have it, we can go on making it. Finally, whether or not a work

of art is feigned or imagined is irrelevant if the art is good. . . . What is art? Art is energy shaped by intelligence.
— GORE VIDAL, *Matters of Fact and Fiction*, 1977

371. The poet is in the end probably more afraid of the dogmatist who wants to extract the message from the poem and throw the poem away than he is of the sentimentalist who says, "Oh, just let me enjoy the poem."
— ROBERT PENN WARREN, "The Themes of Robert Frost," Hopwood Lecture, 1947

372. I have delayed writing because each time I have put pen to paper the letter has increased itself into a half-finished essay on poetry.
— DOROTHY WELLESLEY, Letter to W. B. Yeats, June 11, 1935

373. A poem compresses much in a small space and adds music, thus heightening its meaning.
— E. B. WHITE, *Here Is New York*, 1949

374. We Poets in our youth begin in gladness;
But thereof come in the end despondency and madness.
— WILLIAM WORDSWORTH, *Resolution and Independence*, 1802

375. To read a poem like prose, that hearers unaccustomed to poetry may find it easy to understand, is to turn it into bad, florid prose.
— WILLIAM BUTLER YEATS, *Modern Poetry*, 1936

376. Sometimes I have regretted destroying all that poetry I worked on for so many years, but now I believe I was right.
— KATHERINE ANNE PORTER, "Berlin 1931," in *Collected Essays*, 1970

377. The essential difficulty for the poet in the present age is not that he has some peculiar experience which others do not have. No, all of us, readers and non-readers alike, are in the same boat. We all have experiences of the sacred, but fewer and fewer of them are public, so that the present-day reader of poetry has to translate a poem into his own experience before he can understand it in a way that readers in earlier times did not.

Before people complain about the obscurity of modern poetry, they should, I think, first ask themselves how many profound experiences they themselves have really shared with another person. One further point. I am inclined to think that the rhythmical character of poetry is, in a technological civilization, an obstacle. Rhythm involves

repetition and today I fear that the notion of repetition is associated in
most people's minds with all that is most boring and lifeless....
—W. H. AUDEN, remarks at the National Book Awards,
quoted in *The New York Times*, November 11, 1986

378. Between the self and the terrible world comes poetry with its
minute redemptions, its lyrical insurgencies, its willing suspension of
disbelief in tomorrow.
—TERRENCE DES PRES, *Praises and Dispraises:*
Poetry and Politics, 1988

379. Osric, a poet
Oswald, an advertising man
Osric: My hair is falling out, and no one reads my poems.
Oswald: My liver is bad, and everyone reads my ads.
Osric: Alas I am marginal to the economy.
Oswald: Alas, I am central to the economy.
Osric: Of course, you had to sell your soul.
Oswald: And you were unable to sell yours.
—HOWARD NEMEROV, "The Poet and the Copy-Writer, a Dialogue,"
The Nation, Vol. 183, No. 19, November 10, 1956

380. The poet turned critic is faced with the novel danger of con-
tradicting himself.
—C. DAY LEWIS, "The Poetic Image," Clark Lectures, 1946

381. Most poems, translated to a sunlit street, would be acts of
gross indecency.
—JOHN ASH, "Twentieth Century," *The New Yorker*, July 29, 1991

382. So my poem is damned, and immortal fame is not for me!
—HERMAN MELVILLE, *The Fiddler*, 1854

• Prefaces,
Quotations, Others •

383. Half my friends disapprove of the title I have chosen for this
book without having read it.
—HAROLD ACTON, *Memoirs of an Aesthete*, 1948

384. Three things must epigrams, like bees, have all
A sting, and honey, and a body small.
—ANONYMOUS, quoted in the *Norton Introduction to Literature*, 1977

385. P. S. I have never read a preface in my life, and I suppose you will not read this.
—HILAIRE BELLOC, Preface to *This and That and the Other*, 1912

386. Quotation, *n.* The act of repeating erroneously the words of another.
—AMBROSE BIERCE, *The Devil's Dictionary*, 1911

387. Forewards, as a rule, I detest, since in nine times out of ten, they are either an apology or an admission that something that should have been said in the text has been omitted. Moreover, I have never come across any one except myself who reads them.
—STURTHUS BURT, *The Other Side*, 1928

388. Presumption or meanness are both too often the only articles to be discovered in a preface.
—GEORGE CRABBE, Preface to *Inebriety: A Poem*, 1775

389. It is a good thing for an uneducated man to read books of quotations. *Bartlett's Familiar Quotations* is an admirable work, and I studied it intently. The quotations when engraved upon the memory give you good thoughts. They also make you anxious to read the authors and look for more.
—WINSTON CHURCHILL, *My Early Life*, 1930

390. A preface is an invention to enable an author to argue with his critics without disturbing the general reader, who is expected to skip the preface.
—SHERWIN CODY, Preface to *A Selection from the Best English Essays*, 1903

391. What is an epigram? a dwarfish whole,
Its body brevity, and wit its soul.
—SAMUEL TAYLOR COLERIDGE, *What Is an Epigram?*, 1802

392. I have refrained almost entirely from quoting remembered sayings by George Eliot, because it is difficult to be certain of complete accuracy, and everything depends on accuracy.
—J. W. CROSS (Husband of George Eliot), Introduction of *Eliot's Journal*, "How I Came to Write Fiction," December 1884

393. I knew that there ought not to be any preface to this book, that it would spoil it, and I said so. But people would not believe me, and so here I am, despite myself, launched on a gratuitous and graceless undertaking in which I am sure to please nobody.
— ANATOLE FRANCE, Preface to *Jeunes Madames* by Brada

394. I have heard that nothing gives an author so great pleasure as to find his works respectfully quoted by others.
— BENJAMIN FRANKLIN, *The Way to Wealth*, 1758

395. One standard ploy is to say so much in a dedication that the author says nothing. . . . This approach seems motivated by fear more than anything else — fear that one will never write another book.
— JOHN MAXWELL HAMILTON,
New York Times Book Review, April 15, 1990

396. The epigraph for this chapter has not yet been written.
— ELIZABETH JANEWAY, Epigraph to
Chapter 20 of *Powers of the Weak*, 1980

397. Take away from most of our works on morality the "Advertisement to the Reader," the "Epistle Dedicatory," the "Preface," the "Table of Contents," and the "Permission to Print," and there will scarcely be pages enough left to deserve the name of a book.
— LA BRUYÈRE, *Characters*, 1688

398. The fourth class comprises the following miscellaneous powers.
1. A power "to promote the progress of science and useful arts, by securing for a limited time, to writers and inventors, the exclusive right, to their respective writings and discoveries."
— JAMES MADISON, *The Federalist* #43, January 23, 1788

399. I have decided to quote your own words, so you cannot complain I am distorting your argument.
— SIR THOMAS MORE, Letter to a Monk, John Batmanson, 1519

400. He may also be entertained by learning the sayings of famous men.
— QUINTILIAN, Book I, i, 36

401. Any translator will appreciate the advantage of working on a medieval text. There are no nasty copyright problems.
— NORMAN SHAPIRO, *The Comedy of Eros*, 1970

402. An author's quote quotient depends upon two things: the quotability of the work itself and our ability to quote it. Half of quotability lies in the text, half in the reader.

—GARY TAYLOR, "Brush Up Your Shakespeare,"
New York Times, July 22, 1990

403. I have the sin of translation on my conscience. As poet's eunuch the translator sometimes has pretensions.

—JOHN WARDEN, *Fallax Opus*, 1980

404. You haven't read it! Why! It's wonderful! It's superb! It's immense! You have no idea what you have missed. And the author! Ah! He is divine.

—JACK WOODFORD, *Evangelical Cockroach*, 1929

• Words •

405. The lover of words for their own sake often finds himself in a jungle. There is a great mystery in the way words meet each other in rhymes and puns, like amorous couples of the most diverse origin.

—HAROLD ACTON, *Memories of an Aesthete*, 1948

406. I have become so lonely
　　that only the word
　　is free enough and large enough to take my
　　　mind off
　　the world going day
　　by day over the brink
　　used up but unused...

—A. R. AMMONS, *The Snow Poems*, 1977

407. The criterion of logos, coherent speech, is not truth or falsehood but meaning. Words as such are neither true nor false. The word "centaur" for instance ... means something, though nothing true or false, unless one adds "non-being" or "being" to it. Logos is speech in which words are put together to form a sentence that is totally meaningful by virtue of synthesis (syntheke). .... In the urge to speak is the quest for meaning, not necessarily, the quest for truth. .... In any case, since words—carriers of meaning—and thoughts resemble each other, thinking beings have an urge to speak, speaking beings have an urge to—think.

—HANNAH ARENDT, *The Life of the Mind, One/Thinking*, 1978

408. The words themselves of the Latin tongue, both theological and philosophical, were brought in for the most part from other languages; of which words the Latins suspect some to be from another tongue, while others they do not consider as descending from such a source. Many, in fact, are reckoned as wholly Latin when in reality they are Greek or Hebrew, Arabic or Chaldean . . . for it is no small impropriety to make mistakes in words; because as a consequence a man errs in his statements, then in his arguments, and at length in what he reckons as conclusions. For Aristotle says, "Those who are ignorant of the meaning of words often reason falsely."
— ROGER BACON, "Study of Tongues," *Opus Majus*, 1267

409. I wish there were some words in the world that were not the words I always hear.
— DONALD BARTHELME, *Snow White*, 1967

410. Only the words break the silence.
— SAMUEL BECKETT, *Texts for Nothing* 8, 1958

411. Words are but little bubbles thrown up to express what lies below, forever inexpressible.
— HENRY WARD BEECHER, *Notes from Plymouth Pulpit*, 1865

412. The enemies of "and" will have it that a good style in English is to be obtained by cutting out "and." These are the same people who say that a good style is to be obtained by cutting out adjectives.
— HILAIRE BELLOC, on "And" from *On*, 1923

413. Seeing comes before words.
— JOHN BERGER, *Ways of Seeing*, 1972

414. If the reader of literature is to understand what a writer says, he must understand the writer's words.
— RALPH PHILIP BOAS, *The Study and Appreciation of Literature*, 1931

415. For your born writer, nothing is so healing as the realization that he has come upon the right word.
— CATHERINE DRINKER BOWEN, *Adventures of a Biographer*, 1946

416. Roper: There's to be a new Act through Parliament, sir!
More: Act?
Roper: Yes, sir — about the marriage!
More: Oh.

Margaret: Father, by this Act, they're going to administer an oath.
More: An oath! On what compulsion?
Roper: It's expected to be treason!
More: What is the oath?
Roper: It's about the marriage, sir.
More: But what is the wording?
Roper: We don't need to know the wording—we know what it will mean!
More: It will mean what the words say. An oath is MADE of words. It may be possible to take it. Or avoid it.
More: . . . You want me to swear to the Act of Succession?
Margaret: "God more regards the thoughts of the heart than the words of the mouth" or so you've always told me.
More: Yes.
Margaret: Then say the words of the oath and in your heart think otherwise.
More: What is an oath than but words we say to God?
More: . . . when a man takes an oath, Meg, he's holding his own self in his own hands.
—ROBERT BOLT, *A Man for All Seasons*, Act 2, 1960

417. I turned from side to side, from
image to image, to put you down,
All to no purpose; for you the
rhymes would not sing.
—LOUISE BOGAN, "Poem in Prose" in *The Blue Estuaries*, 1968

418. Human beings have a wholly unique gift in the use of language, and that is that they talk to themselves. Everybody does it, all the time. At this moment every one of you is carrying on an internal dialogue and a considerable part of it is actually taking place in words. You have a lot of irrelevant thoughts about what you are going to wear tonight or where you are going to be . . . but you do not put such thoughts into words because they are not specific, you are just conscious that you are thinking about how much longer without actually saying it to yourself. [There is] a gift linguists usually call the productivity or generality of language. Because of this strange gift one can say "John loves Lucy" and "Lucy loves John" and, at least in a language like English which does not have any exterior signs of cases, they are indistinguishable except that the words are in a different order and the phrases mean different things . . . by and large and keeping to the simple outline, this structure in human language is unique.
—JACOB BRONOWSKI, *The Origins of Knowledge and Imagination*, 1978

419. In reading, when I come upon an unfamiliar word or phrase I have a sensation of derailment.

—ROGER BROWN, *Words and Things*, 1958

420. A very strange inversion . . . to read of things to understand words, instead of learning words that we may be the better enabled to profit by the excellent things which are wrapped up in [them].

—EDMUND BURKE, letter to Richard Shacketis and Richard Burke, July 25, 1746

421. A very great part of the mischiefs that vex the world arise from words. People soon forget the meaning, but the impression and passion remain.

—EDMUND BURKE, letter to Richard Burke, quoted by Gerald W. Chapman in *Edmund Burke*, 1967

422. Words are like money; there is nothing so useless, unless when in actual use.

—SAMUEL BUTLER, *The Notebooks of Samuel Butler*, 1912

423. But words are things, and a small drop of ink, falling like dew, upon a thought, produces that which makes thousands, perhaps, millions, think.

—LORD BYRON, *Don Juan* III, 88, 1819

424. Words mean more than we mean to express when we use them: so a whole book ought to mean a great deal more than the writer meant.

—LEWIS CARROLL, letter to the Laurie children, August 18, 1884

425. "When I use a word," Humpty Dumpty said in a rather scornful tone, "it means just what I choose it to mean—neither more nor less."
"The question is," said Alice, "whether you can make words mean so many different things."

—LEWIS CARROLL, *Through the Looking Glass*, 1871

426. In the course of . . . evolution, words are reduced more and more to the status of mere conceptual signs.

—ERNST CASSIRER, *Language and Myth*, 1946

427. Words are the symbols we use to call things; indeed, we call them, we evoke them.

—PAUL CLAUDEL, *Poetic Art*, 1948

428. [A man] has no way of judging men unless he understands words.

— CONFUCIUS, *The Analects*, Book XX, 3

429. By power of words gone things revive.

— JOHN DEWEY, Poem 75 (1910–1918)

430. Words have clearly defined dictionary meanings which give the illusion of exactness.

— RENÉ DUBOS, *Reason Awake*, 1970

431. The words to the songs aren't written out just for the paper, they're written so you can read [them]. . . . It ain't the melodies that're important, man, it's the words.

— BOB DYLAN, *Dylan*, 1984

432. The Preacher sought to find pleasing words, and uprightly he wrote words of truth.

— ECCLESIASTES 12:10

433. Words move, music moves
Only in time; but that which is only living
Can only die. Words, after speech, reach
Into the silence. . . . Words strain,
Crack and sometimes break, under the burden,
Under the tension, slip, slide, perish,
Decay with imprecision, will not stay in place,
Will not stay still.

— T. S. ELIOT, "Burnt Norton," *Four Quartets*, 1935–1942

434. There are words which give life
And there are innocent words.

— PAUL ELUARD, *Gabriel Peri*, 1944

435. The human voice is sublime when it clothes wisdom, passion, poetry, in words.

— RALPH WALDO EMERSON, Journal VI

436. Only convertive words can discolor what passes for "reality" to show us the real, what sanctified "reality" hides, the totality hidden or mutilated by conventional (not to say convenient) logic. Convertive words are the enemy, words that neither divert nor advert but, perhaps, convert. These are the words that in today's world are impossible or that, if we try to make them possible, are repressed.

— CARLOS FUENTES, "The Enemy: Words"
in *Literature in Revolution*, 1972

437. Obviously no one can fully appreciate a good poem without understanding the language in which it is written as well as one understands one's native tongue. Perhaps some musicality came through when you hear a poem recited in a unfamiliar language, but you miss all the sorcery—all the ways in which the sound patterns intensify the meanings conferred on the words by a culture, especially the overtones that spring from subtle associations of words with other words and phrases.

One of the saddest aspects of poetry is that as words slowly alter their meanings and pronunciations there is an inevitable erosion of a poems's beauty. . . . A few years ago, while reading a new edition of the collected works of [Emily] Dickinson, I came upon an unfinished poem in which she refers to a tiger's "mighty balls." It took me several minutes to realize she meant his eyeballs, though here, perhaps, it was Emily's ignorance of uncouth slang rather than a change in language that turned the line into a joke.

—MARTIN GARDNER, *The Whys of a Philosophical Scrivener*, 1983

438. One help alone I possessed . . . and that help was the native instinct that warned me, unfailingly, "This is not right! That word will not do."

—ELLEN GLASCOW, *The Woman Within*, 1955

439. I hate to see a parcel of big words without anything in them.

—WILLIAM HAZLITT, "On Familiar Style" from *Table Talk*, 1821

440. Our teaching is too full of words, and they come too soon.

—JOHN HOLT, *Why Children Fail*, 1964

441. You will express yourself right well indeed
If by an artful junction you succeed
In giving common words a novel air.

—HORACE, *The Art of Poetry*, circa 17 B.C.

442. Dictionaries are but the depositories of words already legitimatized by usage. Society is the work-shop in which new ones are elaborated. When an individual uses a new word, if illinformed it is rejected in society, if wellinformed, adopted.

—THOMAS JEFFERSON, letter to John Adams, August 15, 1820

443. There is but one word, Mr. President, in the paper which I disapprove, and that is the word "Congress"; on which Ben Harrison rose and said, "There is but one word in the paper, Mr. President, of which I approve, and that is the word "Congress."

—THOMAS JEFFERSON, remarks attributed to John Dickerson
Autobiography of Thomas Jefferson, June 1775

444. The difficulty with many words is that they have a relative
rather than an absolute, or a subjective rather than an objective significance; that is, their exact meaning is dependent on circumstances, or
upon the person who uses them, or on the context in which they are
used.
—R. W. JEPSON, *Clear Thinking*, 1936

445. Write in a book all the words that I have spoken to you.
—JEREMIAH 30:2

446. You must never put two words or lines where one will do; the
age is too busy and hurried to stand it.
—CHARLES KINGSLEY, *Advice to an Author*, 1848

447. I figure language is a poor enough means of communication
as it is. So we ought to use well the words we've got. Besides there are
damned few words that everybody understands.
—JEROME LAWRENCE and ROBERT E. LEE,
Inherit the Wind, Act I, Scene 2, 1955

448. You never pushed a noun against a verb except to blow up
something.
—JEROME LAWRENCE and ROBERT E. LEE,
Inherit the Wind, Act III, 1955

449. There has been a devastation of words.... A lot of words
need a long vacation.
—JACKSON LEARS, *U.S. News and World Report*,
December 5, 1983

450. As an aficionado of literature it might interest you to know
that in all of Shakespeare, the word assertive appears not a single time.
—FRAN LEBOWITZ, *Metropolitan Life*, 1974–1978

451. Words, words, words,
I'm so sick of words
I get words all day through
First from him now from you
Is that all you blikers can do.
—ALAN JAY LERNER, "Show Me" in *My Fair Lady*, 1959

452. Now there are no more words, I bring a leaf, a flower, and a stone.

    —ANNE MORROW LINDBERGH, *The Unicorn*, 1956

453. Conrad spent a day finding the *mot juste*; then killed it.

    —ROBERT LOWELL, Ford Maddox Ford
in *Notebook 1967–1968*

454. Sentences and words are a passion and they do not just happen they evolve gradually.

    —MARTY MARTIN, *Gertrude Stein
Gertrude Stein Gertrude Stein*, 1979

455. Words can sting like anything.

    —PHYLLIS MCGINLEY, *The Love Letters
of Phyllis McGinley*, 1954

456. "The unconscious geniuses of the people," said Paul Shorey, "no more invents slang than it invents epics. It is coined in the sweat of the brow by smart writers who, as they would say, are out for the 'coin'."

    —H. L. MENCKEN, "American Slang" from
The American Language, 1936

457. Socrates: You mean words can't picture reality at all?
Mantias: That's what I mean.

    —IRIS MURDOCH, *Acastos, a Dialogue About Art*, 1986

458. There is no more reason to believe that all words fall naturally into right parts of speech than there is to think that silver comes naturally in either dollars or shillings.

    —L. M. MYERS, *The Roots of Modern English*, 1966

459. Poetry seemed mostly a matter of words: you used obscure, shocking or archaic words; you juxtaposed them in unexpected ways, and the meaning took care of itself.

    —JAN NOVAK, "The Typewriter Made Me Do It,"
New York Times, April 2, 1989

460. There is much evidence that it is virtually impossible to exhaust the wealth of meaning in words, especially root words, and to paraphrase them precisely.

    —JOSEF PIEPER, *Belief and Faith*, 1963

461. Socrates: I can't help feeling, Phaedrus, that writing is unfortunately like painting; for the creations of the painter have the attitude of life, and yet if you ask them a question they preserve a solemn silence ... and when [the speeches] have been once written down they are tossed about anywhere among those who do not understand them. And they have no reticences or proprieties towards different classes of persons; and, if they are unjustly assailed or abused, their parent is needed to protect his offspring, for they can not protect or defend themselves. ... Imagine another kind of writing or speaking far better ... intelligent writing which is graven in the soul of him who has learned ... he will not seriously incline to unite them in water with pen and ink or in dumb characters which have not a word to say for themselves and can not adequately express the truth.
— PLATO, *The Phaedrus*

462. Words are like leaves; and where they most abound
Much fruit of sense beneath is rarely found.
— ALEXANDER POPE, *An Essay
on Criticism*, II, 309–310, 1709

463. Before a word is even on my tongue, you know it.
— PSALM 139: 4

464. Words: the pieces of change in the currency of a sentence.
They must not get in the way. There is always too much small change.
— JULES RENARD, "Diary," April 1908

465. Human reaction to words, like much other human behavior, is also motivated by irrational impulses.
— LOUIS B. SOLOMON, *Semantics and Common Sense*, 1966

466. Be careful of words...
Words and eggs must be handled with care.
Once broken they are impossible
things to repair.
— ANNE SEXTON, "Words" in
The Awful Rowing Toward God, 1975

467. Polonius: What do you read my Lord?
Hamlet: Words, words, words.
— SHAKESPEARE, *Hamlet*, II, ii

468. Many writers have employed themselves to small purpose in ridiculing each other's notions, and in wasting time in the investigation of a few isolated words, instead of setting steadily to work to analyse the whole of them.

> —WALTER W. SKEAT, "Essay on the Rowley Poems,"
> Political Works of Thomas Chatterton, 1891

469. Words are the signs of ideas, and when the ideas are huge, sometimes disordered and endlessly ramified, none but the patient craftsman who cares naught for space or time will catch their meaning.

> —GERARD S. SLOYAN, "Thomas Wolfe: A Legend of a Man's Youth
> in His Hunger" in Fifty Years of the American Novel, 1957

470. I mould my words, snatched from the clutch of gods,
Upon the glowing gold of the noontide sun.

> —ANTONIN SOVA, The Poet, 1906

471. The art of literature stands apart from among its sisters, because the material in which the literary artist works is the dialect of life; hence, on the one hand, a strange freshness and immediacy of address to the public mind, which is ready prepared to understand it; but hence, on the other, a singular limitation. The sister arts enjoy the use of a plastic and ductile material, like the modeler's clay; literature alone is condemned to work in mosaic with finite and quite rigid words . . . since these blocks, or words, are the acknowledged currency of our daily affairs, there are here possible none of those suppressions by which other art obtains relief, continuity, and vigor; no hieroglyphic touch, no smoothed impasto, no inscrutable shadow, as in painting; no black wall, as in architecture; but every word, phrase, sentence, and paragraph must move in a logical progression, and convey a definite conventional import.

> —ROBERT LOUIS STEVENSON,
> Essays of Travel and In The Art of Writing, 1905

472. I have written something like 35,000 words since I have been here, which shows at least I have been industrious.

> —ROBERT LOUIS STEVENSON, letter to
> Charles Baxter, November 1818

473. The man who agrees with my meaning; agrees with my words.

> —ST. AMBROSE, Exposition of St. Luke 2:42

474. In the beginning was the Word.

> —ST. JOHN, Gospel, 1:1

475. The dialogue is short, sharp, and continuous. It is broken by the minimum of description and by no preaching. It is almost entirely in slang of the most exaggerated kind.
—WILLIAM GRAHAM SUMNER, *What Our Boys Are Reading,* 1880

476. It's strange that words are so inadequate.
—LEONARD UNGER, epigraph to *T. S. Eliot: Moments and Patters,* 1966

477. These ten English words are used far more frequently than any others; a, and, I, in, is, it, of, that, the, to.
—HUGH WALPOLE, *Semantics,* 1941

478. It is the tragedy of the lexicographer that new words come into existence or earlier information comes to hand while his work is in the press.
—ERNEST WECKLEY, *Something About Words,* 1935

479. There is no word for "word" in Chinese.
—BENJAMIN LEE WHORF, "A Brotherhood of Thought," in *Main Currents in Modern Thought,* 1941

480. Hemingway was, without any question, the greatest; he had a poet's feeling for words, economy.
—TENNESSEE WILLIAMS, *Playboy,* April 1973

481. Words, those small bricks with which we would build the cuts.
—WILLIAM CARLOS WILLIAMS, "An Approach to the Poem," *English Institute Essays,* 1947

482. From the time he was first able to remember, all the way back to when words weren't words but colors and images of states of mind, what he remembered most of all was the qualities of the stories.
—LARRY WOIWODE, *Beyond the Bedroom Wall,* 1975

483. I would hurl words into this darkness and wait for an echo, and if an echo sounded, no matter how faintly, I would send other words to tell, to march, to fight, to create a sense of hunger for life that gnaws in us all.
—RICHARD WRIGHT, *American Hunger,* 1977

484. "I have heard," said Socrates, "of certain words that have all the force in them of the most powerful charms."
—XENOPHON, *Memoirs of Socrates*

485. I feel that one's verse must be as direct and natural as spoken words.
— W. B. YEATS, letter to Dorothy Wellesley, July 26, 1935

486. It's the words that sing, they soar and descend . . . I bow to them . . . I love them, I cling to them, I run them down, I bite into them, I melt them down.
— PABLO NERUDA, "The Word (A Prose Poem)" from *Lives on the Line: The Testimony of Contemporary Latin American Authors*, 1988

487. English words are the right and proper names which acts were meant to have, and all other words but pitiable failures. How could one improve upon splash, smash, ooze, shriek, slush, glide, squeak, coo? Who could think of anything more sloppy than slop? Is not the word sweet a kiss in itself?
— WILLIAM RALPH INGE, *More Lay Thoughts of a Dean*, 1931

• Writers •

488. Most English authors are miserly talkers: either they refuse to take the trouble or they are busy making mental notes, or they are shy.
— HAROLD ACTON, *Memoirs of an Aesthete*, 1948

489. He had so well mixed and digested his knowledge of men and books, that he made one of the most accomplished persons of his age.
— JOSEPH ADDISON, "The Education of an Heir," *The Spectator*, No. 123, July 21, 1711

490. I have observed that whenever a Boston author dies, New York immediately becomes a great literary center.
— THOMAS BAILEY ALDRICH, *Ponkapog Papers*, 1902

491. Why do so many people want to be writers anyway?
— SHERWOOD ANDERSON, "When the Writer Talks," *Literary Review*, 1925

492. Three things are necessary for becoming a writer: a good head, a thick skin, and a soft heart.
— AUSTIN J. APP, *The Way to Creative Writing*, 1954

493. My mother's diary was written in gall. . . . When I finished reading it I burned it, and I tried to forget it.
—MARY ASTOR, *My Story: An Autobiography*, 1959

494. It has been said that his childhood is a writer's entire capital.
—LOUIS AUCHINCLOSS, *A Writer's Capital*, 1974

495. There are people who are too intelligent to become authors.
—W. H. AUDEN, "Reading," *The Dyer's Hand*, 1962

496. It is harder for an American than it is for a European to become a good writer, but if he succeeds, he contributes something unique; he sees something and says it in a way that no one before him has said it.
—W. H. AUDEN, on Henry James, in
Introduction to *The American Scene*, 1946

497. [The writer] is here to describe things which other people are too busy to describe.
—JAMES BALDWIN, *Notes for a Hypothetical Novel*,
October 22, 1960

498. God wasn't too bad a novelist, except he was a Realist.
—JOHN BARTH, interview in *Wisconsin Studies
in Contemporary Literature* 6, 1965

499. On the day when a young writer corrects his first proof-sheet he is as proud as a schoolboy who has just got his first dose of the pox.
—CHARLES BAUDELAIRE, "My Heart Laid Bare,"
in *Intimate Journals*, 1864

500. Music is the catalytic element in the work of Proust.
—SAMUEL BECKETT, *Proust*, 1931

501. Writing men work in part for fame . . . some perhaps among the greatest have the attainment of fame for their whole motive.
—HILAIRE BELLOC, *On Translation*, 1931

502. I never considered it a duty to write about the fate of the Jews. I didn't need to make that my obligation. I felt no obligation to write—what I was really moved to write.
—SAUL BELLOW, interview in
Bostonia, November/December 1990

503. The fact that there are so many weak, poor and boring stories written and published in America has been ascribed by our rebels to the horrible squareness of our institutions, the idiocy of power, the debasement of sexual instincts and the failures of writers to be alienated enough. The poems and novels of these same rebellious spirits, and their theoretical statements, are grimy and gritty and very boring too, besides being nonsensical, and it is evident now that polymorphous sexuality and vehement declarations of alienation are not going to produce great works of art either. There is nothing left for us novelists to do but think. For unless we think, unless we make a clearer estimate of our condition, we will continue to write kid stuff, to fail in our function, we will lack serious interests and become truly irrelevant.

—SAUL BELLOW, remarks at National Book Awards, quoted in *New York Times*, November 16, 1986

504. Nothing is easier, unfortunately, than to be deceived about the true character of an author who is still living. Most of our books, in fact, do not take on their true significance until after we are dead.

—GEORGE BERNANOS, *France Before the World of Tomorrow*, 1947

505. I have always been puzzled by the idea that we writers should lay down our sense of good and evil before we take up our pens.

—BJØRNSTJERNE BJØRNSON, acceptance of Nobel Prize, 1903

506. There are some [novelists and dramatists] who become really obsessed by their hero; it is he who controls them, not they who control him; they even have difficulty in getting rid of him when they have finished their play or their novel.

—HENRI BERGSON, *The Two Sources of Morality and Religion*, 1932

507. When a writer has been brought to a halt by death, one kind of activity in him has to replace another: he can no longer cover more ground, like a tractor; he has to work upon us with a static persistence, like an electric drill.

—ELIZABETH BOWEN, on Conrad in *The Spectator*, September 1936

508. Neither my experience, my acquirements, nor my powers are sufficiently varied to justify my ever becoming a frequent writer.

—CHARLOTTE BRONTË, Letter to G. H. Lewis, January 12, 1848

509. [Freud] is a writer who has been vastly discussed by millions who never looked at a line he ever wrote.

—HEYWOOD BROUN, *It Seems to Me*, 1925–1935

510. The kind of scrutiny a writer brings to other people both complicates and enhances friendship. It is his peculiar fate to see more than he can bear. You are, in his eyes, at once insufficient as a character and excessive.
—ANATOLE BROYARD, "Writers Beware Writers,"
New York Times, May 21, 1989

511. A ream of fresh paper lies on my desk waiting for the next book, I am a writer and I take up my pen to write.
—PEARL BUCK, *My Several Worlds*, 1954

512. Some intelligent people are turning to the older novelists.
—DOUGLAS BUSH, "Sex in the Modern Novel,"
Atlantic, January 1959

513. The first thing a young writer must expect and yet can least of all suffer, is criticism. . . . The best replies to all objections is to write better and if your enemies will not then do you justice, the world will. On the other hand, you should not be discouraged; to be opposed is not to be vanquished, though a timid mind is apt to mistake every scratch for a mortal wound. There is a saying of Dr. Johnson's . . . "no man was ever written down except by himself. . . ."
—LORD BYRON, letter to John Hamilton Reynolds, February 20, 1814

514. Shakespeare's name, you may depend on it, stands absurdly too high and will go down. . . . He took all his plots from old novels, and threw their stories into a dramatic shape, at as little expense of thought as you or I could turn his plays back into prose tales.
—LORD BYRON, 1814

515. Like all other artists, writers are not "made." Samuel Butler advised a young man "who wanted to write" that he was too late: Writers are born.
—TAYLOR CALDWELL, "The Essence of Good Writing,"
in *The Writer's Handbook*, 1964

516. Writers, most of all, need to define their tasks . . . I mean particularly the defining of their themes, their objections.
—HENRY SEIDAL CANBY, *Definitions*, 1922

517. Movies about writers tend to fall to pieces when the writers start writing. . . . The act of writing is private, and whether it's done with a quill pen or a personal computer, it is singularly uninvolving to the looker-on.
—VINCENT CANBY, *New York Times*, October 4, 1990

518. For the last decade or so I prefer writers I've already read. Proven wine.
—TRUMAN CAPOTE, *The Dogs Bark*, 1973

519. Most writers, like most men, are not strong enough to bear complete liberty.
—DAVID CECIL, "Anthony and Cleopatra,"
W. P. Ker Memorial Lecture, University of Glasgow,
1943, in *Poets and Storytellers*, 1948

520. I assumed the burden of a profession, which is to write even when you don't want to, don't much like what you are writing, and aren't writing particularly well.
—AGATHA CHRISTIE, *Autobiography*, 1977

521. A really good writer is always a modern writer, whatever his century.
—MARCHETTE CHUTE, *Geoffrey Chaucer*, 1946

522. No man of genius ever wrote for the mob; he never would consciously write that which was below himself. Careless he might be, or he might write at a time when his better genius did not attend him, but he never wrote anything that he knew would degrade himself.
—SAMUEL TAYLOR COLERIDGE, "Lecture on Shakespeare 9," 1812

523. If any man on earth more than another needs to be true to himself as he hopes to be saved, it is certainly to the writer of fiction.
—JOSEPH CONRAD, *A Personal Record*, 1912

524. He has no reputation as a historian to lose, and [his historical book] can only enhance his standing as a writer of fiction.
—ALBERT COWDREY, on James Bacque's book *Other Losses*
quoted in *New York Times Book Review*, February 24, 1991

525. It is clear enough that to be a son of a novelist of growing reputation has its drawbacks.
—GORDON A. CRAIG, about Golo Mann, reviewing
*Reminiscences and Reflections, New York Times
Book Review*, September 16, 1990

526. A writer looking for subjects inquires not after what he loves best, but after what he alone loves at all.
—ANNIE DILLARD, "Write Till You Drop,"
New York Times, May 28, 1989

527. You know who the critics are? The men who have failed in literature and the arts.
— BENJAMIN DISRAELI, *Lothair*, Vol. II, Chapter 4

528. Someone once said: "The dead writers are remote from us because we know so much more than they did." Precisely, and they are that which we know.
— T. S. ELIOT, *The Sacred Wood*, 1920

529. The more perfect the artist, the more completely separate in him will be the man who suffers and the mind which creates; the more perfectly will the mind digest and transmute the passions which are its material.
— T. S. ELIOT, "Tradition and the Individual Talent,"
in *The Sacred Wood*, 1920

530. You do not write a novel for praise, or thinking of your audience. You write for yourself; you work out between you and your pen the things that intrigue you.
— BRET EASTON ELLIS, *New York Times*, March 6, 1991

531. My enemies tried to destroy my career, but they couldn't. They destroyed more easily the lives of people in the movie business because they were part of an industry. But with a writer, it is more difficult. You only need paper and a pencil. So, I kept writing, sometimes using pseudonyms, and I never gave up.
— HOWARD FAST, interview in *Press-Republican*,
Plattsburgh, New York, January 20, 1991

532. By artist I mean of course everyone who has tried to create something which was not here before him, with no other tools and material than the uncommerciable ones of the human spirit; who has tried to carve, no matter how crudely, on the wall of that final oblivion, in the tongue of the human spirit, "Kilroy was here." That is primarily, and I think in its essence, all that we ever really tried to do. And I believe we will all agree that we failed. That what we made never quite matched and never will match the shape, the dream of perfection which we inherited and which drove us and will continue to drive us, even after each failure, until anguish frees us and the hand falls still at last.
— WILLIAM FAULKNER, remarks at the National Book Awards (1955)

533. The mature writer must write, as he has always written, for neither mass nor sect but for that pure fiction, the ideal understander,

for whom we no longer have a name but who was once called the "gentle reader."
— LESLIE FIEDLER, *An End to Innocence*, 1955

534. I had been lucky enough to improve the method or the language, and this encouraged me to think I might possibly in time come to be a tolerable English writer, of which I was extremely ambitious.
— BENJAMIN FRANKLIN, *Autobiography*, 1771

535. He that can compose himself, is wiser than he that composes books.
— BENJAMIN FRANKLIN, *Poor Richard's Almanac*, 1732–1757

536. The writer does the same as the child at play; he creates a world of phantasy which he takes very seriously.
— SIGMUND FREUD, *The Poet and Day-Dreaming*, 1908

537. I was born a novelist, though I formed myself into an artist.
— ELLEN GLASCOW, *The Woman Within*, 1955

538. A great writer meets more than one requirement, answers more than one doubt, satisfies various appetites.
— ANDRÉ GIDE, *Pages from the Journal*, 1909

539. Rage is to writers what water is to fish.
— NIKKI GIOVANNI, *Sacred Cows and Other Edibles*, 1988

540. No one in his right mind would ask a teenager to write or evaluate his life.
— NIKKI GIOVANNI, *Sacred Cows and Other Edibles*, 1988

541. The primitive need of the writer—to know, to master, to tell—has recaptured his intentions about himself.
— HERBERT GOLD, *First Person Singular*, 1963

542. It is in some ways a melancholy thought that I have become a school textbook before I am properly dead and buried.
— WILLIAM GOLDING, "Fable" in *The Hot Gates*, 1966

543. Occupation: Writer. . . . This is how I fill in my income-tax return—but cynically because "writer" has become almost meaningless as a descriptive term.
— ROBERT GRAVES, *Occupation: Writer*, 1950

544. He was a writer and far too imaginative to settle for the simple facts.

—HELEN HAYES on Charles MacArthur
in *On Reflection: An Autobiography*, 1968

545. It is the deepest desire of every writer, the one we never admit or even dare to speak of; to write a book we can leave as a legacy. And although it is sometimes easy to forget, wanting to be a writer is not about reviews or advances or how many copies are printed or sold. It is much simpler than that, and much more passionate. If you do it right, and if they publish it, you may actually leave something behind that can last forever.

—ALICE HOFFMAN, "The Book That Wouldn't Die,"
in *New York Times Book Review*, July 22, 1990

546. The writer does not get from his work as he writes and reads it the same aesthetic shock that the reader does.

—RANDALL JARRELL on Erskine Caldwell
in *Southern Review* 1, 1935–1936

547. One was not allowed to read everything. For a long time Aarestrup's poems and Oehlenschläger's "Aly and Gulhyndy" were forbidden—though only with result that both were read in secret.

—JOHANNES JÖRGENSEN, *An Autobiography*, 1916

548. And being a novelist, I consider myself superior to the saint, the scientist, the philosopher, and the poet, who are all great masters of different bits of man alive, but never got the whole hog.

—ALFRED KAZIN quoting D. H. Lawrence,
in the epigraph to *Bright Book of Life*, 1971

549. Every religious author is *eo ipso* polemical; for the world is not so good that the religious man can assume that he has triumphed or is in the party of the majority.

—SØREN KIERKEGAARD, *The Point of View
for My Work as an Author*, 1848

550. A shallow mind thinks his writing divine; a man of sense imagines he writes tolerably well.

—LA BRUYÈRE, *Characters*, 1688

551. I have been thinking about writing a pseudonymous novel for years. Like, I am sure, most writers.

—DORIS LESSING, Preface to *The Diaries of Jane Somers*, July 1984

552. Today we are all looking for darkness visible, and we know that a realistic awe of evil is a mighty valuable thing for a writer to have.
— ROBERT LOWELL, *Art and Evil*, 1955

553. The writer is like a person trying to entertain a listless child on a rainy day.
— JOHN D. MACDONALD, "Creative Trust"
in *The Writer's Handbook*, 1977

554. I am a frustrated writer, as all my life I've been chasing good literature no matter who wrote it and trying to find if the person was alive, so that I could talk about it with him.
— JACK MACGOWAN, in "MacGowan on Beckett,"
Theater Quarterly, 3 (II, July-Sept., 1973)

555. Ultimately, novelists must believe that the people who run the world are essentially good, are an expression of God's work . . . or in antithesis must decide that the Devil is at the shoulder of every ruler.
— NORMAN MAILER, *Cannibals and Christians*, 1966

556. Now, really, what is it that I do want to write? I ask myself, am I less of a writer than I used to be? Is the need to write less urgent?
— KATHERINE MANSFIELD, *Journal*, January 22, 1916

557. Oh, to be a writer, a real writer given up to it and to it alone.
— KATHERINE MANSFIELD, *Journal*, February 29, 1920

558. "One would have to be a saint . . . but then one would not write novels." There, in two lines, is the whole debate of Mauriac. But of course one would. One would write novels if one were born a novelist. . . . Saints have been kings, artists, preachers, doctors, priests, painters, poets. Why should they not be novelists?
— JACQUES MARITAIN, quoting François Mauriac in
Creative Intuition in Art and Poetry, 1943

559. Those who write only for money, and who would cease to write if they have enough without it, I don't consider writers at all.
— DON MARQUIS, *Saturday Review of Literature*, 1932

560. To their credit, most Irish writers have consistently kept up their resistance to all the direct and indirect constraints on expression.
— D. E. S. MAXWELL, *Brian Friel*, 1973

561. The odds against an unknown author getting a manuscript published by simply sending it to a publishing house are astronomical.
— EDWIN MCDOWELL, *New York Times*, January 29, 1982

562. I wish another writer would have written it, I mean a writer who'd never written of fathers and sons.
— ARTHUR MILLER, on *All My Sons*,
interview with Ronald Hayman, February 15, 1969

563. There are a great many people who really believe in answering letters the day they are received, just as there are people who go to the movies at 9 o'clock in the morning; but these people are stunted and queer.
— CHRISTOPHER MORLEY, "On Unanswering Letters"
in *Mince Pie*, 1919

564. He was either a good writer who wrote bad books or a bad writer who wrote good books.
— WILLIE MORRIS, on James Jones' critics'
remarks in *James Jones, a Friendship*, 1978

565. The great writer does not really come to conclusions about life; he discerns a quality in it.
— J. MIDDLETON MURRY, *The Problem of Style*, 1922

566. The theory that a playwright is necessarily and inevitably a writer is advanced by people with no education in etymology.
— GEORGE JEAN NATHAN, *The Theater Book of the Year*, 1950–1951

567. He seized a pen and paper,
Set down everything he knew,
And re-united God and devil, since
He shared all secrets common to the two.
— ALDEN NOWLAN, "The Drunken Poet"
in *Playing the Jesus Game*, 1970

568. Self-criticism is an art not many are qualified to practice. Despite our best efforts it is probable that, apart from the most immediate, pragmatic, technical revisions, the writer's effort to detach himself from his work is quixotic: knowing too much is a way of knowing too little; or, conversely, how can we expect to know more about ourselves than we know about anything else . . . . We are all in the position of King Lear, who holding absolute authority over his kingdom, "but slenderly knew himself." . . . The writer must accept it as a premise of his existence that certain delusions—one of these, in fact, the delusion of "self-knowledge"—are necessary for his career; as necessary as delusions of various sorts are for all of us. . . . We must hold [the principle that] if we are to survive as writers, deluded or otherwise [that] we are steadily improving; whatever we are working on at the present time is the best thing we have ever done. . . . All writers are quintessentially American—we fear that not to progress is to plunge into the abyss. And we may be right.

—JOYCE CAROL OATES, "The World's Worst Critics,"
New York Times Book Review, January 18, 1987

569. Nothing, it seems, can obliterate the worthless writer short of a world-war. And more go on appearing every week of the year from some of our best publishers.

—SEAN O'FAOLAIN, *The Short Story*, 1951

570. In all but a few Italian novelists . . . is there anything but a rampant delight in carnal love?

—SEAN O'FAOLAIN, *A Summer in Italy*, 1948

571. A portrait, like a novel, is a fiction. In the compact between novelist and reader, the novelist promises to lie, and the reader promises to allow it. . . . Literary essayists, critical and social thinkers, historians, journalists and so forth don't in general, or at least not ideally, set out to defraud. The essayist's contract is exactly contrary to the novelist's—a promise to deliver ideas and "issues," implicit in which is a promise to show character. Fiction writers may easily begin as persons of character—more easily, say, than political columnists who are tempted to put a finger lightly on the scale—but the likelihood is that in the long run fiction bruises character. Novelists invent, deceive, exaggerate and impersonate for several hours every day and frequently on the weekends. Through the creation of bad souls they enter the demonic as a matter of course. They usurp emotions and appropriate lives.

—CYNTHIA OZICK, "Good Novelists, Bad Citizens,"
in *The New York Times*, February 15, 1987

572. A busy age will hardly educate its writers in correctness. Let its writers make time to write English more as a learned language.

—WALTER PATER, *English Literature*, Feburary 17, 1886

573. The only thing I can pass on to a younger writer is that: read.

—WALTER PERCY, interview in
The Charlotte Observer, September 30, 1962

574. All the writers the students were supposed to mimic wrote without rules, putting down whatever sounded right, then going back to see if it still sounded right and changing it if it didn't. There were some who apparently wrote with calculating premeditation because that's the way their product looked.
— ROBERT M. PIRSIG, *Zen and the Art of Motorcycle Maintenance*, 1974

575. It has seemed to us that a publisher's first allegiance is to talent, which is very rare and valuable.
— MAXWELL PERKINS, letter to a writer, November 13, 1944

576. Writers have been killed by politicians for expressing certain ideas or writing in certain ways; but (what is less often acknowledged) these same politicians have also been inspired by other writers to shed the blood of their fellow-writers, and millions of non-writers as well.
— NORMAN PODHORETZ, *The Bloody Crossroads*, 1986

577. It would be nice indeed if cultural and social crisis could be solved or ameliorated by more and closer reading of the "elder writers." Most writers, most readers even more so, want to believe in such magnifications of literary method and literary meaning. The belief is essential to the notion that the writing and reading of literature have a culturally redemptive power. I am arguing that this belief cannot be sustained by the actual operations of language in literary texts. Writing that can be called literature tends to be discernibly on edge about its own rhetorical status, especially when the rhetoric is conspicuously indebted to any of the great, historically rooted institutions, as in the theological-mystical-literary saturations of idiom in "Paradise Lost" and "Ulysses." Part of the excitement of such works derives from the way they resist as well as absorb the meaning which their adopted language makes available to them, and to us.
— RICHARD POIRIER, "Why Literature Can't Save Us," *New York Times Book Review*, February 8, 1987

578. Why did I write? What sin to me unknown
Dipped me in ink, my parent's or my own.
— ALEXANDER POPE, *Epistle to Dr. Arbuthnot*, 1734

579. In every work regard the writer's end,
Since none can compass more than they intend.
— ALEXANDER POPE, *An Essay on Criticism*, 255–256, 1709

580. We should read none save the best authors and such as are least likely to betray our trust in them.

— QUINTILIAN, Book X, i, 20

581. It is apparent that she has suffered during the writing of this book.

— DUDLEY RANDELL, on Sonia Sanchez in
Introduction to *We a BaddDDD People*, 1970

582. So a novelist is the same as a journalist, then. Is that what you are saying?

— JUDGE WILLIAM J. REA, his question during
the MacDonald-McGinniss trial, July 7, 1987;
epigraph in Janet Malcolm's *The Journalist and
the Murderer*, 1990

583. As a writer, I try to set limits for myself. As a reader I set no limits.

— JULES RENARD, *Journal*, April 1895

584. One can quickly discover if a poet has talent. In the case of prose writers, it takes a little longer.

— JULES RENARD, *Journal*, December 1903

585. And then I begin to work. I was riding the crest of inspiration. Everything suddenly took form, and the words came. I was still deep in the guilt phase (of my mother's death) . . . and being able to write at such a time only served to exacerbate that guilt, as a matter fact. But who knows? Greater writers by far have suckled long and deep on guilt, and mankind has been nourished and blessed for it. The writing, when it came, was an intensely physical event. My temperature went down. I was cold, always cold. The fingers that held the pen were stiff. . . . Writers of fiction occasionally talk about their books or characters as independent beings, unfolding on their own as the work progresses, surprising their author with shenanigans and their fates . . . as my novel developed, I discerned emerging from its paper in bolder and more vivid colors as theme that, of course, I had put there myself.

— TORA REICH, "My Mother, My Muse" in
The New York Times Magazine, November 6, 1988

586. In order to read properly what one has written, one must think it again.

— JULES RENARD, "Diary," January 1909

587. A lady in a green dress asks, "Didn't we meet at the Thompson's party last month in Malibu?"

And, "What do you do, Mr. Rodriquez?"

I write: I am a writer.

A part time writer. When I began this book, five years ago, a fellowship bought me a year of continuous silence in my San Francisco apartment. But the words wouldn't come.

—RICHARD RODRIQUEZ, *Hunger of Memory,*
An Autobiography, 1982

588. In Eastern Europe a man should be more careful of what he writes, even to his girl friend.

—PHILIP ROTH, on Milan Kundera's *The Joke, Esquire,* April 1974

589. Should the writer teach English composition or shouldn't he? Should the writer accept the money of some dead tycoon or shouldn't he? Is it worse from a dead tycoon or a live tycoon? Should the writer smoke marijuana or shouldn't he? Can he survive in New York? Is Yaddo bad for you? Should he have a telephone?

The concern is with writers instead of writing; the concern is with poses and postures, with etiquette; it is as if the manners of the writer ultimately determined the manner of the writing.... As writers, and not as question-answerers, it is only in our worst moments that we display so simplified an attitude toward the multiplicity of human response and human personality. Why should we permit our inquisitors to make us talk like the characters we create when art and understanding fail us?

—PHILIP ROTH, remarks at National Book Awards,
quoted in the *New York Times,* November 16, 1986

590. For a country that has always had a strong sense of tradition it is astonishing how little Irish writers have delved into the past as a subject for books.

—DIAMUID RUSSELL, *Portable Irish Reader,* 1946

591. The extreme wickedness of reviewers has been a conviction with many authors—who have sometimes, it would seem, succumbed to it themselves and retaliated in reviewing others.

—GEORGE SAINTSBURY, *A Letter Book,* 1922

592. Fain would I woo her, yet I dare not speak;
I'll call for pen and ink, and write my mind.

—SHAKESPEARE, I *Henry VI,* V, iii

593. He hath never fed of the dainties that are bred in a book;
He hath not eat paper, as it were;
He hath not drunk ink; his intellect is not replenished.
— SHAKESPEARE, *Love's Labour's Lost,* IV, ii

594. I used to sit in the bathroom with the running water in the sink and write because the echo against the tile was nice.
— PAUL SIMON, songwriter, interview in
Gannett Newspapers, October 11, 1990

595. You evidently possess, and in no inconsiderable degree, what Wordsworth calls the "faculty of verse."
— ROBERT SOUTHEY, letter to Charlotte Brontë, March 1837

596. I have learned something when I realize that what I most wanted out of life was to write my own stuff.
— STEPHEN SPENDER, letter to
Christopher Isherwood, August 3, 1939

597. The difference between the writer of serious fiction and the writer of escape entertainment is the clear difference between the artist and the craftsman.
— WALLACE STEGNER, "Fiction: A Lens on Life,"
Saturday Review, 1950

598. The fiction writer is an incorrigible lover of concrete things.
— WALLACE STEGNER, "Fiction: A Lens on Life,"
Saturday Review, 1950

599. It is often necessary for a writer to distort the particulars of experience in order to see them better.
— WALLACE STEGNER, "Fiction: A Lens on Life,"
Saturday Review, 1950

600. It often happens that criticism, and especially criticism of Shakespeare, is mainly interesting for the light which it throws upon the critic.
— LYTTON STRACHEY, "Shakespeare on Johnson,"
The Spectator, August 1, 1908

601. This massive concentration on a handful of writers (for reasons all too often nonliterary), coupled with a massive exclusion of

most other writers from consideration, can result in a ludicrously distorted picture of the American literary situation.
— HARVEY SWADOS, "Must Writers Be Characters?"
Saturday Review, XLIII, October 1, 1960

602. A true critic in the perusal of a book, is like a dog at a feast, whose thoughts and stomach are wholly set upon what the guests fling away, and consequently, is apt to snarl most, when there are the fewest bones.
— JONATHAN SWIFT, *A Tale of a Tub*, 1750

603. Many a distinguished author in his advanced years has completely revised the entire body of his work, usually for the worse.
— JAMES THURBER, *The Beast in Me and Other Animals*, 1949

604. To decry commercialization but accept the money characterizes too many authors today, and in my view, that's hypocritical.
— SCOTT TUROW, attributed by Roger Cohen,
New York Times, March 25, 1990

605. I like everything there is about being a writer except the way my neighbors treat me.
— KURT VONNEGUT, JR., interview in the *New Fiction* 1974

606. At this stage the furniture of his mind was as a sediment whirling muddily in a carrying fluid, and many years passed before it settled down sufficiently to allow him to start out on his career as a writer.
— EDWARD SACKVILLE-WEST, *Thomas De Quincey*, 1936

607. The revelation of an overlooked genius is always a pleasure, since it reveals not only the excellence of our own taste but also the obtuseness of someone else.
— ANNA MARY WELLS, "Early Criticism of Emily Dickinson,"
American Literature, Vol. I, No. 3, November 1929

608. I have sometimes had the experience of picking up from him some idea that I thought was particularly illuminating and introducing it into something I was writing, only to be told by the sage himself that this had not been at all what he meant, that he had, in fact, meant the opposite.
— EDMUND WILSON, *Upstate*, 1957

609. I cannot tell any one how to write books; I cannot attempt to give any one rules whereby he will be enabled to get his books published by publishers or his stories accepted by high-paying magazines. I am not a professional writer; I am not even a skilled writer; I am just a writer who is on the way to learning his profession and to discovering the line, the structure, and the articulation of the language which I must discover if I do the work I want to do. It is for just this reason, because I blunder, because every energy of my life and talent is still involved in this process of discovery, that I am speaking as I speak here. I am going to tell the way in which I wrote a book.

—THOMAS WOLFE, *The Story of a Novel*, 1936

610. I believed for the first time that I could actually be a writer. I did not see myself as one of those lofty authors who sit at a typewriter and do not move their lips—but I could be funny on paper and had proved it. . . . At last I was learning how to tap the big balloon in a misshapen body—learning how to put a tube down into it, so the foolishness came flying out onto a piece of paper.

—JOAN RIVERS, *Enter Talking*, 1986

611. If we accept the truism that all writers are voyeurs, then we can say that an hour a day in a confined space like a church, where one has the leisure or the boredom to observe others of one's kind when they imagine themselves; to be in private communication with their deepest souls, is as useful for a prospective novelist as a wiretap. Daily Mass was the home ground of the marginal, the underemployed; you always wondered why they weren't at work or getting ready for work. A child at daily Mass got to observe at close range the habits of old women, of housewives at eight-thirty already tired out for the day, men down on their luck praying for a reversal of their bad fortunes.

—MARY GORDON, in *Spiritual Quests: Art and Craft of Religious Writing*, 1988

612. Recent writers on metaphor often insist, sometimes in extravagant terms, on the power of metaphors. They also complain about the prejudice against metaphor that springs, they suggest, from a narrow, literalist (positivist) conception of language. The fact of the matter is that the vast majority of metaphors are routine and uninteresting. Many metaphors are lame, misleading, overblown, inaccurate, et cetera. Metaphors, in indicating that one thing is like another, so far say very little. Their strength, which they share with comparisons in general, is that their near-emptiness makes them adaptable for use in a wide variety of contexts. On the reverse side, the near-emptiness

also makes them serviceable for those occasions when we want to avoid saying, and perhaps, thinking, what we really mean. Euphemisms are typically couched in metaphors. Metaphors can be evasions—including poetic evasions.
— ROBERT J. FOGELIN, *Figuratively Speaking*, 1988

613. Every author has a meaning which reconciles all contradictory passages, or else he has no meaning at all.
— BLAISE PASCAL, *Pensées*, Section I, XIX, 1659

614. It wasn't a practiced writer
You guessed—from the way the sentence toiled.
— EMILY DICKINSON, Poem #494

615. Many writers learn to handle the idolatry of their fans with a measure of grace, but if you are a writer who has the misfortune to be dead as well as famous, matters are less under your control.
— JULIAN BARNES, "The Follies of Writer Worship,"
New York Times Book Review, 1985

616. It's appropriate to pause and say that the writer is one who, embarking upon a task, does not know what to do.
— DONALD BARTHELME, "Not-Knowing," *Georgia Review*, 1985

617. If something comes into a writer's or painter's mind the only thing to do is to try it, to see what one can do with it, and give it a chance to show if it has real value. Story-telling is always experimental.
— SARAH ORNE JEWETT, letter to Miss Rose Lamb, September 11, 1896

618. The truth is that the world's great writers are apt to become the world's great bores.
— LOGAN PEARSALL SMITH, "On Reading Shakespeare," 1933

619. How DeLillo contrives to fashioning interesting novels from material like this is always a puzzle, since he seems so indifferent to most of the textbook principles of storytelling—things like "character development," plots that reward expectations, verisimilitude to ordinary experience.
— LOUIS MENAND, on *Mao II* by Don DeLillo,
The New Yorker, June 24, 1991

620. He preferred the backlist of any dead writer to the stress and tension of trying to deal with a live one.
— MAVIS GALLANT, "Forain," *The New Yorker*, June 24, 1991

• Writing •

621. So often is the virgin sheet of paper more real than what one has to say, and so often one regrets having marred it.
—HAROLD ACTON, *Memoirs of an Aesthete*, 1948

622. A pen is certainly an excellent instrument to fix a man's attention and to inflame his ambition.
—JOHN ADAMS, diary, November 14, 1760

623. I am writing this book to please myself. It likely may not, and I have no idea whether it will please anyone else. The point is I want to clarify something in my own mind.
—JAMES TRUSLOW ADAMS, *The American*, 1944

624. My idea is to keep an even tone of rough and ready realism in all the subordinate parts of a story, rising to the lyric, or impassioned when the event demands: at such moments permitting myself all the beauty I'm capable of. I allow myself slang, and all blunt, ordinary words that have meanings.
—CONRAD AIKEN, letter to Grayson McCouch, December 1912

625. Good writing is making yourself a clear transparency for an idea worth writing about.
—JANET AIKEN, "Good and Bad Grammar,"
The American Mercury, November 1932

626. I think we owe it to our children to get back to talking and writing English, but we're not going to do it with lazy expressions.
—ROBERT THOMAS ALLEN, *Children,
Wives, and Other Wildlife*, 1970

627. Writer: The ending.
Actor: Of course. What are we discussing? We're discussing the ending.
Writer: We're always discussing the ending.
Actor: Because it's hopeless.
Writer: I admit it's unsatisfying.
Actor: Unsatisfying? It's not even believable. The trick is to start at the ending when you write a play. Get a good strong ending and then write backwards.
Writer: I've tried that. I got a play with no beginning.

Actor: That's absurd.
Writer: Absurd? What's absurd?
Actor: Every play must have a beginning, middle and end.
Writer: Why?
Actor: Because everything in nature has a beginning, middle and end.
Writer: What about a circle?
— WOODY ALLEN, "God, a Play" from *Without Feathers*, 1975

628. She was already in the habit of writing down important matters, and afterward, when she was mute, she also recorded trivialities, never suspecting that fifty years later I would use her notebooks to reclaim the past and overcome terrors of my own.
— ISABEL ALLENDE, *The House of the Spirits*, 1985

629. You may write me down in history,
With your bitter, twisted lies,
You may trod me in the very dirt
But still, like dust, I'll rise.
— MAYA ANGELOU, "And Still I Rise," 1978

630. Revising and updating a book is always a blessing because it not only ministers to the editor's heart, it also breathes new life into a nineteenth century message which might otherwise be overlooked by the twentieth century reader.
— ANONYMOUS, Publishers Note for Andrew Murray's
The Master's Indwelling, 1983

631. o shit that I could carve
words in contours
of voluptuous breasts...
o fuck I wish
I could write like that
— ANONYMOUS, Dedication of *Outsider* #4/5, Winter 68-69

632. There is no crispness about it and the action is not quick enough, a serious charge to make against a book of adventure.
— ANONYMOUS, Review of Joseph Conrad's *An Outcast of the Islands*
in *National Observer*, Vol. 15, April 18, 1896

633. In literary composition there is only one fundamental principle: clarity. Nothing else is as vital as that. . . . There is no good writing that is not clear. There is no clear writing that is not good.
— BROOKS ATKINSON, *Once Around the Sun*, 1951

634. How he found time to write so many letters to so many people was always a mystery because all of the letters were tossed off with style.
— BROOKS ATKINSON, on Sean O'Casey,
New York Times, September 22, 1964

635. Edith [Wharton] shows herself [in these early stories] already in full command of the style that was to make her prose as lucid and polished as any in American fiction. It is a firm, crisp, smooth, direct, easily, flowing style, the perfect instrument of a clear, undazzled eye, an analytic mind, and a sense of humor. . . . The defect in Edith's poetry is that this same style, consciously ennobled and stripped of laughter, became dull and ornamental. Prose was always her natural instrument . . . [she] would create a wholly sympathetic novelist character who deliberately uses every emotional experience, however personal, however intimate, as grist for her fictional mill. She knew that thus novels are made.
— LOUIS AUCHINCLOSS, *Edith Wharton,
a Woman in Her Time*, 1971

636. When a successful author analyses the reasons for his success, he generally understands the talent he was born with, and overestimates his skill in employing it.
— W. H. AUDEN, "Writing," *The Dyer's Head*, 1962

637. If a man write little, he had need have a great memory.
— FRANCIS BACON, "On Studies," 1597

638. I have loved writing, especially in the winter, early in the morning, sitting with my back to the fireplace at a card table. . . . It has taken me two years to trace these threads of my personal, political, spiritual and musical lives — how they came together and how they fell apart . . . I am recording them for myself, to take a hard look before facing forward in these most bizarre of times.
— JOAN BAEZ, *And a Voice to Sing With*, 1987

639. Don't you think it would make your tough guys a little more interesting to the reader if once in a while you had one bend down to smell a rose.
— RUSSELL BAKER, advice to him from Elliot Coleman
in *Growing Up*, 1982

640. I have in my time filled many hundred sheets with my useless

scribble, the greater part of which I will commit to the flames shortly, to prevent their giving me any uneasiness in my last moments.
—GEORGE BALLARD, letter to Dr. Lyttelton, May 22, 1753

641. Mr. DeMarinis's truck [taking the narrator on a journey] is that this is done with enormous affection and without irony: it is pure and ancient comedy. We who have identified with the narrator join him on his amazing journey: he has become for us a reliable witness to a ridiculous, utterly unbelievable series of events composed of the details of everyday life, the same details of everyday life, the same details that make the stories of Richard Ford and Raymond Carver, for example, so believable. But while their stories, like Hemingway's, so often leave one face to face with the everyday and loving it mainly for its esthetic possibilities, Mr. DeMarinis leaves one facing that humdrum reality filled with belief in one's ability to transcend it. . . . His language is demotic: he has a gifted ear for American speech, a crush on all kinds of slang, and usually relies on a first-person narrator. He has a wry appreciation of brand names, the details of contemporary life, but unlike the so called minimalists, he refuses to use them as a short-hand method for characterization and instead uses them to show how his characters are diminished by their material lives.
—RUSSELL BANKS, New York Times, October 30, 1988

642. How do you turn catastrophe into art? Nowadays the process is automatic. A nuclear plant explodes? We'll have a play on the London stage within a year. A President is assassinated? You can have the book or the film or the filmed book or the booked film. War? Send in the novelists. A series of gruesome murders? Listen for the tramp of the poets. We have to understand it, of course, the catastrophe, however minimally. Why did it happen, this mad act of Nature, this crazed human moment? Well, at least it produced art. Perhaps, in the end, that's what catastrophe is for.
—JULIAN BARNES, A History of the World in 10½ Chapters, 1989

643. Some disquieting confessions must be made in printing at last the play of Peter Pan; among them this, that I have no recollection of having written it.
—J. M. BARRIE, The Dedication of the Play (circa 1928)

644. I have made this longer only because I did not have the leisure to make it shorter.
—JOHN BARTH, Letters, 1979, quoting Blaise Pascal,
Lettres Provinciales XVI

645. It seems a long time since the morning mail could be called correspondence.
— JACQUES BARZUN, *God's Country and Mine*, 1954

646. Inspiration comes always when man wills it, but it does not always depart when he wishes.
— CHARLES BAUDELAIRE, *Les Fleurs du Mal*, 1857

647. To write a pot-boiler, that is genius.
— CHARLES BAUDELAIRE, *Les Fleurs du Mal*, 1857

648. Whoever writes maxims likes to exaggerate his character — the young pretend to be old, the old paint their faces.
— CHARLES BAUDELAIRE, *Les Fleurs du Mal*, 1857

649. One is exhausted and angry after an hour, submerged, dominated by the crest and break of metaphor after metaphor; but never stupefied.
— SAMUEL BECKETT, *Proust*, 1931

650. Journals are often the devil's vanity trap. Men write in them pretending to themselves that they don't expect them to be published, when all the time they know that they will be; and are writing under the influence of that idea.
— HENRY WARD BEECHER, *Notes from Plymouth Pulpit*, 1865

651. We are all writing books — histories of our own lives, and we can omit nothing.
— HENRY WARD BEECHER, *Notes from Plymouth Pulpit*, 1865

652. I had rather written one of Charles Wesley's hymns than to have built the proudest monument in Egypt.
— HENRY WARD BEECHER, *Notes from Plymouth Pulpit*, 1865

653. Like most people who are in the habit of writing things to be printed, I have not the knack of writing good letters.
— MAX BEERBOHM, *How Shall I Word It?*, 1910

654. I have heard ascribed to myself in my own presence sharp little verses which I never wrote. And to some of them I have had to say, "Would that I had written them!" though to others I have had to say, "No, thank God, I did not write them."
— HILAIRE BELLOC, *Short Talks with the Dead and Others*, 1926

655. An ability to cut, revise and center your own work, that is one of the most valuable things any writer can learn and that an awful lot of writers (young ones especially) never go to the trouble of learning.
— STEPHEN VINCENT BENÉT, letter to George Abbe, 1935

656. I wrote another story yesterday and am typing it today . . . I do not see how it can fail to sell—it is so cheap.
— STEPHEN VINCENT BENÉT, letter to
Rosemary Benét, May 25, 1926

657. I certainly felt when I had finished that I never wanted to write another line as long as I lived—and yet I won't be sad to start this new novel when I do.
— STEPHEN VINCENT BENÉT, letter to
his mother, November 5, 1927

658. Yesterday I began to think that the tone of the end of my novel wouldn't do. So I spent the day . . . generally thinking over the climax.
— ARNOLD BENNETT, *Journal*, April 20, 1917

659. The pupils at the Royal Military College were now the most extraordinary crowd. Poets and novelists pullulated among them.
— ARNOLD BENNETT, *Journal*, April 12, 1917

660. [Tom Jones] is equal to its reputation; consistently interesting. There is no dull chapter. But he makes it too good.
— ARNOLD BENNETT, *Journal*, August 19, 1911

661. Nothing could prevent me from finishing that novel [*A Great Man*]. I was in the exact mood for writing, and had all the ideas arranged in my head.
— ARNOLD BENNETT, *Journal*, March 13, 1904

662. Novel, *n*. A short story padded.
— AMBROSE BIERCE, *The Devil's Dictionary*, 1911

663. It was here, in this noisome place, in spite of all I had read and been taught and thought I knew about it before, that the mysterious, awful power of writing first dawned on me.
— ELIZABETH BISHOP, *The U.S.A. School of Writing*, 1966

664. Writing isn't your career, it's your religion. Writing is your form of prayer. You put words together one by one to reach the truth.
— MARY KAY BLAKELY, comment to her sister, Gina Blakely, in *Wake
Me Up When It's Over*, 1989

665. I've never been a fan of oral history, finding the spoken word leaden and clumsy in print. Depending on written speech rather than prose is essentially risky.
— MARY KAY BLAKELY, *New York Times*, April 29, 1990

666. A play is a team game. Otherwise, go away and write a novel.
— ALAN BLEASDALE, Author's Note in *Are You Lonesome Tonight?*, 1985

667. After living as a writer for many years, I have noticed that a pattern made up of the supporting writing, as it were, begins to show itself.
— RONALD BLYTHE, *Characters and Their Landscapes*, 1983

668. The best time to write about one's childhood is in the early thirties, when the contrast between early forced passivity and later freedom is marked.
— LOUISE BOGAN, *Journey Around My Room*, 1980

669. A hundred times consider what you've said:
Polish, repolish, every color lay,
And sometimes add, but oft'ner take away.
— BOILEAU, *The Art of Poetry*, 1683, lines 170–172

670. In writing vary your discourse and phrase.
— BOILEAU, *The Art of Poetry*, 1683, line 70

671. The only literary sin of any importance is to dilute one's originality. And that dilution, in some graceful and accepted form, is the aim of nine hundred writers out of a thousand.
— ELIZABETH BOWEN, quoting G. W. Stonier in a review of *The Shadow Across the Page* in *The New Statesman and Nation*, 1937

672. I think I want to write a book about what it is like to be a professional athlete in America.
— BILL BRADLEY, *Life on the Run*, 1976

673. I must have my own way in the matter of writing.
— CHARLOTTE BRONTË, letter to W. S. Williams, September 21, 1849

674. Easy writing makes damned hard reading.
— RUPERT BROOKE, "Democracy and the Arts," Paper to Cambridge University Fabian Society, 1910

675. To select is to distort.
— MATTHEW BRUCCOLI, Editorial Note
in James Cozzens' *Notebooks*, 1984

676. Everything that interrupts the interest, everything that destroys the scenic illusion, all that is merely fine and showy, must be retrenched without mercy.
— WILLIAM CULLEN BRYANT, *North American Review*, Vol. XI

677. Thus I set Pen to Paper with delight,
And quickly had my thoughts in black and white.
For having now my Method by the end,
Still as I pulled, it came; and so I penned it down.
— JOHN BUNYAN, *The Pilgrim's Progress*, 1678

678. By the time one has finished a piece it has been so often viewed and reviewed before the mental eye, that one loses, in a good measure, the powers of critical discrimination. Here the best criterion I know is a friend.
— ROBERT BURNS, letter to Dr. John Moore, January 4, 1789

679. The moment a thing is written, or even can be written, and reasoned about, it has changed its nature by becoming tangible, and hence finite.
— SAMUEL BUTLER, *The Notebooks*, 1912

680. Fiction does best when taught to look like truth.
— LORD BYRON, *Hints from Horace*, 1821

681. What had made the novel so hopeless was that I didn't seem to have the least idea where I was going with it, or even which paragraph should follow which. But my short stories, which were put into the mouth of some character, marched right along . . . and knew perfectly well what they had to say.
— JAMES M. CAIN, Introduction to *Three of a Kind*, August 24, 1942

682. The art of writing, like every other art, is simpler in practice than the books about it.
— HENRY SEIDAL CANBY, *Better Writing*, 1926

683. In a way I used up some of my loneliness by writing.
— TRUMAN CAPOTE, attributed to him in a review of *The Words of Truman Capote* in the *Times Literary Supplement*, July 27, 1973

684. It took five years to write *In Cold Blood*, and a year to recover — if recovery is the word; not a day passes that some aspect of that experience doesn't shadow my mind.
— TRUMAN CAPOTE, *The Dogs Bark*, 1973

685. My only advice farther in regard to your studies, is that when you read you take pains to reflect well also; and that when you write, you be not too careful of what you shall say, but especially in letters put down the thoughts warm and vivid as they present themselves before your fancy. They often gain in vigor what they want in elegance: besides it is good to be uninteresting even stupid sometimes when we address a friend.
— THOMAS CARLYLE, letter, December 4, 1822

686. Do not say you cannot: write as you used to write in those delightful cunning little lively epistles you send me, and the thing we want is found. I too will write in my own poor vein, neither fast nor well, but steadfastly and stubbornly: in time we shall both improve: and when we have enough accumulated for a volume, then we shall sift the wheat from the chaff . . . a man must write a cart-load of trash, before he can produce a handful of excellence.
— THOMAS CARLYLE, letter, December 16, 1822

687. My great anxiety is to get my book done, before bodily and mental powers begin to fail.
— LEWIS CARROLL, letter to Mrs. Blakemore, February 1, 1888

688. The practice of youthful novel writing has done as much as any other one thing to weaken and vitiate literature.
— WILLA CATHER, *Journal*, October 28, 1894

689. The notion seems to have gone abroad that a man can write before he has lived. . . . The talent for writing is largely the talent for living, and is utterly independent of knowledge.
— WILLA CATHER, *Journal*, October 28, 1894

690. If you have enough talent, you can get by after a fashion without guts; if you have enough guts, you can also get by, after a fashion again, without talent. But you certainly can't get by without either.
— RAYMOND CHANDLER, letter to Carl Brandt, February 13, 1951

691. I would like a more muscular vocabulary. And I must be careful about my cultivated accent. When this gets into my prose, my prose is at its worst.
— JOHN CHEEVER, *Journals*, *The New Yorker*, August 13, 1990

692. It is a good theme [the Steppe] and it is pleasant to work on it, but unfortunately, owing to lack of practice in writing long things, and from fear of crowding in too many details, I go to the opposite extreme: each page comes out compact, like a short story, the pictures multiply and huddle together, and, vying with one another for the reader's attention and interest, they spoil the single impression I wish to attain. As a result one gets, not a picture in which all the details are merged into a whole, like stars in the heavens, but a mere summary, a dry inventory of impressions. A writer—you for instance,—will understand me, but the reader will be bored, and will eschew it all.
—ANTON CHEKHOV, letter to V. G. Korolinko, January 9, 1888

693. There is every type and time of fable: but there is only one moral to the fable; because there is only one moral to anything.
—G. K. CHESTERTON, Introduction to *Aesop's Fables*, 1912

694. Plays are much easier to write than books because you can see them in your mind's eye.
—AGATHA CHRISTIE, *Autobiography*, 1977

695. I've worked for nearly a year on a long poem . . . it's become a great deal longer than I imagined and I am hardly beginning to understand what I wanted to say.
—PAUL CLAUDEL, letter to André Gide, June 10, 1912

696. The rules of the imagination are themselves the very powers of growth and production. The words, to which they are reducible, present only the outlines and external appearances of the fruit.
—SAMUEL TAYLOR COLERIDGE, *Principles of Criticism*, viii, 22, 1817

697. A writer can have limitations, impotences, but also, thank God, a clear conscience.
—COLETTE, letter to Henri Mondor, June 6, 1938

698. I've finished my book . . . as usual, it took days and nights of despair.
—COLETTE, letter to Hélène Picard, November 1931

699. If I don't write it's because I'm writing.
—COLETTE, letter to Marguerite Moreno, September 28, 1925

700. Writing is a design, often a portrait, nearly always a revelation.
—COLETTE, *The Evening Star*, 1945

701. To unlearn how to write, that shouldn't take much time.
— COLETTE, *The Evening Star*, 1945

702. What's that you're writing?
Oh, nothing. I scratch on the paper and then tear it up. When I can't make anything of it, I destroy it.
— COLETTE, *The Evening Star*, 1945

703. In some of my former novels, the object proposed has been to trace the influence of circumstances upon character. In the present story I have reversed the process. The attempt made, here, is to trace the influence of character on circumstances.
— WILKIE COLLINS, Preface to *The Moonstone*, 1868

704. Creative writing is simply writing produced by a creative mind regardless of the form or genre the writer uses for his expression.
— MARY M. COLUM, *From These Roots*, 1937

705. I began to try my prentice hand at various forms of critical writing — for of creative I knew myself incapable — in order to define and if it might be to communciate the pleasures which were to me the salt of life.
— SIR SIDNEY COLVIN, Dedicatory Letter
in *Memories and Notes*, 1852–1912

706. The student should first devote some time to the collection of synonyms, and may then learn to add epithets to nouns, verbs, and adverbs. He may then proceed to the use of antithesis, and later on to that of periphrasis. Then he may substitute figurative words for the originals, alter the order of the words for the sake of euphony, and adorn a simple sentence with all the figures of speech.
— JOHN AMOS COMENIUS, *The Great Didactic*, 1632

707. What I am afraid of is: verbiage.
— JOSEPH CONRAD, letter to Hugh Walpole,
December 2, 1902

708. I begin to fear that I have not enough imagination — not enough power to make anything out of the situation; that I cannot invent an illuminating episode that would set in a clear light the persons and feelings. I am in desperation and I have practically given up the book. Beyond what you have seen I cannot make a step. There are 12 pages written and I sit before them every morning, day after day, for the last 12 months and can not add a sentence, add a word! I am paralyzed by doubt and have just sense enough to feel the agony but am powerless to invent a way out of it. This is the sober truth. I had bad moments with the *Outcast* but never anything so ghastly—nothing half so hopeless. When I face that fatal manuscript it seems to me that I have forgotten how to think—worse! how to write.

—JOSEPH CONRAD, letter to Edward Garnett, August 5, 1896

709. In truth every novelist must begin by creating for himself a world, great or little, in which he can honestly believe.

—JOSEPH CONRAD, *Books*, 1905

710. I have corrected all the "like" into "as" in my copy. One is so strangely blind to one's own prose; and the more I write the less sure I am of my English.

—JOSEPH CONRAD, letter to W. H. Chesson, January 16, 1898

711. ["An Outpost of Progress"] was difficult to write, not because of what I had to write, but of what I had firmly made up my mind not to write into it.

—JOSEPH CONRAD, Preface, March 1906

712. These things happened to them as a warning but they were written down for our instruction.

—1 CORINTHIANS 10:11

713. You are a letter from Christ delivered by us, written not with ink but with the spirit.

—2 CORINTHIANS 3:3

714. I felt fairly wretched but at least relieved that I had had the sense to admit failure . . . facing the fact that my talent had withered and that I should never write any more music.

—NOEL COWARD, *Conversation Piece*, 1934

715. I must face the fact that I find literary and dramatic criticism tedious. . . . I would certainly be interested enough in any proven facts about the causes of a writer's inspiration . . . but I am not interested in the inevitably prejudiced theories of professional critics.

—NOEL COWARD, diary, December 12, 1955

716. The Great American novel, we are assured, can no longer be written on account of the complex variety which has come into American life, making it impossible for one book to mirror all its phases.

—SIR WILLIAM CRAIGIE, *The Making of a Dictionary*,
Saturday Review of Literature, April 21, 1928

717. The inner monologue [of Hawthorne] . . . was the workshop where he forged his plots and tempered his style. Before writing his stories he told them to himself, while walking by the sea or under the pines; he liked a solitary place where there was nothing to distract his attention. . . . "It would suit me to have my daily walk along . . . straight paths," he said in his notebook, "for I think them favorable to thought, which is apt to be disturbed by variety and unexpectedness. . . ." There is more to be said about this inner monologue which played an essential part in his life and work. In one sense it was a dialogue, since Hawthorne seems to have divided himself into two personalities while working on his stories: one was the storyteller and the other his audience. The storyteller uttered his stream of silent words; the audience listened and applauded by a sort of inner glow, or criticized by means of an invisible frown that seemed to say, "But I don't understand. Let me go over it again," and the storyteller would answer, still soundlessly; and then he would repeat his tale in clearer language, with more details.
     —MALCOLM COWLEY, A Many-Windowed House, 1970

718. If you find a lot of explaining necessary, something is wrong with your material or with your approach to it.
     —JAMES GOULD COZZENS, Notebook, July 1, 1960

719. Immediately the fingers of a man's hand appeared and wrote on the plaster of the wall of the king's palace, opposite the lampstand; and the king saw the hand as it wrote . . . the hand was sent, and this writing was inscribed: Mene, Mene, Tekel, and Parsin.
     —DANIEL 5:5

720. "This is one of the many books that I will never write," said D'Annuzio in a letter to his publisher—and enclosed the manuscript.
     —GABRIELE D'ANNUNZIO, quoted by Rudolph Altrocchi
in Sleuthing in the Attic, 1944

721. Dorothy Parker, also a trickler, said: "I can't write five words but I change seven."
     —ROBERTSON DAVIES, A Voice from the Attic, 1990

722. In spite of the part of my life that is turned toward God—or rather, precisely because of this part, which stimulates my inner forces instead of absorbing them—I have need of an "outlet." As I have, unfortunately, no aptitude for either music or poetry, nor even (which I regret most of all) the talent or art of the novelist, I have up to now tried to express myself in all kinds of philosophies—literary essays of which I

have had occasion to show you only an infinitesimal past. Unfortunately, these essays are almost all destined to perish in my desk drawers, or at any rate, to be read only by a limited group of friends.
—PIERRE TEILHARD DE CHARDIN,
Letters to Two Friends (1926–1952)

723. The End, he scrawled, and blotted it. Then eyed
Through darkened glass night's cryptic runes o'erhead.
"My last, and longest book." He frowned; then sighed:
"And everything left unsaid."
—WALTER DE LA MARE, "The Old Author" from
The Burnnig Glass and Other Poems, 1945

724. It was never my intention to write a political book. If my characters are sometimes obliged to speak politically, it is merely an accident.
—MICHEL DEL CASTELLO, Foreword to *The Disinherited*, 1960

725. You shall write upon them all the words of this law.
—DEUTERONOMY 27:3

726. The writer can only explore the inner space of his characters by perceptively navigating his own.
—PETER DEVRIES, quoted in *Without a Stitch in Time*, 1972

727. I'm sure you're tired thinking to yourselves, possibly even murmuring to one another, "This character will talk for half an hour about the creative process, or some such, without telling us a damned thing." I shall not disappoint you.
—PETER DEVRIES, Hopwood Lecture, "Exploring Inner Space,"
1969, quoted in *Without a Stitch in Time*, 1972

728. Again I must say, above all things—especially to young people writing: for the love of God don't condescend! Don't assume the attitude of saying, "See how clever I am, and what fun everybody else is!"
—CHARLES DICKENS, letter to Frank Stone, June 1, 1857

729. I think you are too ambitious, and that you have not sufficient knowledge of life or character to venture on so comprehensive an attempt.
—CHARLES DICKENS, advice to anonymous person
on a novel, letter, February 5, 1867

730. In many ways writing is the act of saying I, of imposing oneself upon other people, of saying listen to me, see it my way, change your mind.
— JOAN DIDION, "Why I Write," *New York Times*, 1976

731. Faulkner's characters impose their nightmare reality upon you because they are built out of truths, the truths of the stirrings of the flesh and blood and passion of real men.
— JOHN DOS PASSOS, *Occasions and Protests*, 1964

732. I defy anybody who has been reading Faulkner to look at a map of the state of Mississippi without expecting to find Yoknapatawpha County there.
— JOHN DOS PASSOS, *Occasions and Protests*, 1964

733. Working for money and working for art are for me incompatible . . . I suffered a great deal because of it. I was loath to prostitute my best ideas and the best plots of my stories and novels by working in a hurry and by having to finish it by a certain date. I loved my characters too much and was anxious to create them without haste, to create them with love. I'd rather have died than dishonor them . . . I did not want to publish anything that was bad, apart from the fact that it would have been dishonest of me to do so. . . . Everything written at one go is immature. Shakespeare, they say, never blotted his manuscripts. That is why there are so many monstrosities and so much bad taste in his plays, whereas had he worked longer at them they would have been much better.
— FYODOR DOSTOEVSKY, quoted by David Magarshack in *Dostoevsky*, 1962

734. If you have that unconquerable urge to write, nothing will stop you from writing. You will write whether it is convenient or inconvenient, whether you are rich or poor, whether you are lonely or your life is filled with friends and frivolity.
— THEODORE DREISER, letter to H. S., September 6, 1929

735. The writer has selected and arranged and lighted his materials in a conscious way; he has deliberately fashioned it for its effect on a public audience. But one form of writing is exempt from this deliberate patterning process: the familiar letter.
— ELIZABETH DREW, *The Literature of Gossip*, 1964

736. That novel is a good novel which succeeds in communicating vividly the writer's experience.
— ELIZABETH DREW, *The Modern Novel*, 1926

737. Learn to write well, or not to write at all.
— JOHN DRYDEN, *An Essay Upon Satire*, 1680

738. He did not mind Alice's having written down so much of this talk — but it was quite another matter to give it the permanence of print.
— LEON EDEL, on Henry James' reaction to his sister's diary, in Preface to *The Diary of Alice James*, 1964

739. Summer had come, the season when I liked to write "literature": it was my way of relaxing, of dreaming, of enjoying vacation time. . . . As usual, I would write from the beginning of the afternoon till evening, then between 11:00 P.M. and 3:00 or 4:00 A.M. I would go to bed at dawn, sometimes after sunrise, and sleep until noon. . . . I was writing with much difficulty, as at other times, but that was not what was bothering me. Rather, it was the tempo of the action, which was too slow. It seemed I was not writing a novel, but a monographic presentation of a group of rather ordinary persons. . . . In one month I wrote about two hundred pages in which almost nothing happened. . . . The original inspiration had begun to fade, and I broke off my writing.
— MIRCEA ELIADE, *Autobiography*, Vol. I, 1981

740. The fact that we die is one of the more interesting things that happen to us. Fiction ought to be about bottom lines, and that's as bottom-line as you can get.
— STANLEY ELKIN, attributed by Ken Emerson in *New York Times*, March 3, 1991

741. Plot is to literature what individual holes are to miniature golf.
— STANLEY ELKIN, attributed by Ken Emerson in *New York Times*, March 3, 1991

742. It has always been a vague dream of mine that sometime or other I might write a novel; and my shadowy conception of what the novel was to be, varied, of course, from one epoch of my life to another.
— GEORGE ELIOT, "How I Came to Write Fiction," *Journal*, 1856

743. Modesty requires me to write briefly; but loyalty requires me to write.
— T. S. ELIOT, Preface to *John Davidson, A Selection of His Poems*, 1961

744. The reason of my success said Garrick to the clergyman is

because I tell fictions as if they were truths and you, truths as if they
were fictions.

— RALPH WALDO EMERSON, *Journal*, VI, 132

745. I only write by spasms, and these ever more rare, and dae-
mons that have no ears.

— RALPH WALDO EMERSON, letter to
Thomas Carlyle, January 23, 1870

746. The writing was the writing of God, graven upon the tables.

— EXODUS 32: 16

747. The cult of "creative writing" is a pretext for avoiding the
labor of organizing one's writing.

— CLIFTON FADIMAN, *Empty Pages*, 1979

748. Our tragedy today is a general and universal physical fear so
long sustained by now that we can even bear it. There are no longer
problems of the spirit. There is only the question: when will I blow up?
Because of this, the young man or woman writing today has forgotten
the problems of the human heart in conflict with itself which alone can
make good writing because only that is worth writing about, worth the
agony and the sweat.
   He must learn them again. He must teach himself that the basest
of all things is to be afraid; and, teaching himself that, forget it forever,
leaving no room in his workshop for anything but the old virtues and
truths of the heart, the old universal truths lacking which any story is
ephermal and doomed. . . .

— WILLIAM FAULKNER, address accepting the Nobel Prize, 1949

749. I learned to read what lay behind the look that veiled people's
faces, I learned how to sketch in human beings with a few rapid words,
I learned to see; to observe, to remember; learned, in short, the first
rules of writing.

— EDNA FERBER, *A Peculiar Treasure*, 1939

750. Any writer whose work, as you read it or hear it, gives you a
fresh and more dimensional impression of life and living, a keener
awareness of the world about you, has that magic sixth sense.

— EDNA FERBER, *A Kind of Magic*, 1963

751. There are no worse men than bad authors.

— HENRY FIELDING, *A Journey from This World to the Next*, 1743

752. When I was at school I had a knack of rhyming, which I unhappily mistook for genius.
—HENRY FIELDING, *A Journey from This World to the Next*, 1743

753. Not having the ability needed to attain success, nor the genius to conquer fame, I am condemned to write solely for myself.
—GUSTAVE FLAUBERT, letter to Louise Colet, October 23, 1846

754. I have never before been so conscious of how little talent is vouchsafed me for expressing ideas in words.
—GUSTAVE FLAUBERT, letter to Louise Colet, April 1847

755. Carefully examined, a good—an interesting—style will be found to consist in a constant succession of tiny, unobservable surprises.
—FORD MADDOX FORD, *Joseph Conrad: A Personal Remembrance*, 1924

756. Let us define a plot. We have defined a story as a narrative of events arranged in their time-sequence. A plot is also a narrative of events, the emphasis falling on causality. "The king died and then the queen died," is a story. "The king died, and then the queen died of grief," is a plot.
—E. M. FORSTER, *Aspects of the Novel*, 1927

757. Unless a man has kept a log book of his voyage, he cannot seize upon each accent of a distant day.
—GENE FOWLER, *Skyline*, 1961

758. I think the first sign that I might one day become a novelist (though I did not then realize it) was the passionate detestation I developed at my own school for all those editions of examinations books that began with a long introduction.
—JOHN FOWLES, *The Tree*, 1979

759. You become a good writer just as you become a good joiner; by planing down your sentences.
—ANATOLE FRANCE, attributed by Jean Jacques Brousson in *Anatole France Himself*, 1925

760. I should have no objection to a repetition of the same life from its beginnings, only asking the advantage authors have in a second edition to correct some faults of the first.
—BENJAMIN FRANKLIN, *Autobiography*, 1771

761. A . . . they say has wit; for what? For writing? No, for writing not.
— BENJAMIN FRANKLIN, *Poor Richard's Almanac* (1732–1757)

762. I cannot write the yellow book you wish me to. I know too little about the human drive for power, for I have lived my life as a theorist.
— SIGMUND FREUD, letter to Arnold Zweig, December 7, 1930

763. I think every writer has had the experience of running up against a type of story which he feels he simply can't write.
— ERLE STANLEY GARDNER, *What's Holding Us Back*, 1952

764. You write what the spirit tells you to, whether the spirit's responsible or not.
— JOHN GARDNER, "John Napper Sailing Through the Universe," in *The King's Indian*, 1972

765. The materials for creative writing are not hard to find. They are right under your nose.
— ROGER A. GARRISON, *A Guide to Creative Writing*, 1951

766. Stanley doesn't just live life. He lives it and then re-forms it in anecdotes.
— WILLIAM GASS, on Stanley Elkin, *New York Times Magazine*, March 3, 1991

767. The expression "to write something down" suggests a descent of thought to the fingers whose movements immediately falsify it.
— WILLIAM GASS, "Habitations of the Word," *Kenyon Review*, Vol. VI, No. 4, October, 1984

768. I date all my work because I think poetry, or any writing, is but a reflection of the moment.
— NIKKI GIOVANNI, *Sacred Cows and Other Edibles*, 1988

769. All of us wrote; poems and stories poured out of us; it was a good thing . . . that the house had so many wastepaper baskets. Where did this passion come from?
— JON AND RUMER GODDEN, *Two Under the Indian Sun*, 1966

770. I had a Wordsworthian belief in the primacy of the lyric. The lyric could be short and simple — the simpler the better.
— WILLIAM GOLDING, "My First Book" from *The Author*, July 1981

771. Sometimes, though, one does reread and realize that something happened that one is glad of. One is tempted to say; "That's pretty good, I wonder who wrote that?" For the reader reading is never the writer writing. One always comes to one's work as a stranger.
—MARY GORDON, *New American Short Stories 2*, 1989

772. The importance of literary criticism in the higher education of a race has been recognized in no country in the world except France.
—EDMUND GOSSE, "Two French Critics"
in *Aspects and Impressions*, 1922

773. Why do I make things more difficult for myself by refusing to write the same sort of book twice?
—ROBERT GRAVES, *Occupation: Writer*, 1950

774. Gene brought four great gifts to journalism—an expanding lump of curiosity, a willingness to listen, a roaring style of writing, and an absolutely natural manner.
—LAWRENCE GREEN, on Gene Fowler, *Esquire*, February 1953

775. As one grows older the writing of a novel does not become more easy, and it seemed to me when I wrote the last words that I had reached an age when another full-length novel was probably beyond my powers.
—GRAHAM GREENE, *In Search of a Character*, 1961

776. All I know about the story I am planning is that a man "turns up," and for that reason alone I find myself on a plane between Brussels and Léopoldville.
—GRAHAM GREENE, *In Search of a Character*, 1961

777. I have to write. It's a bit like shitting. It's quite nice. Especially if you do it nicely . . . if it's coming in drips and drabs or not coming at all, or being forced out, if you're missing the rhythm, it's no pleasure at all.
—GERMAINE GREER, *Playboy*, January 1972

778. I wrote it to free myself. It all happened, and I wrote it on the day it happened, and I had all this garbage in my head that had to be removed before anything else could be written.
—SUSAN GRIFFIN, *Woman and the Creative Process: Lighting the Dark*, 1973

779. I think the only playwrighting rule is that you have to learn your craft so that you can put on stage plays you would like to see. So I threw away all the second acts of the play, started in again, and for the first time, understood what I wanted.
—JOHN GUARE, Introduction to *The House of Blue Leaves*, 1982

780. Write the vision; make it plain upon tablets, so he may run who reads it.
—HABAKKUK 2:2

781. She had written five different endings, and had brought them all, thinking, when the moment came, she would choose one of them.
—LUCRETIA P. HALE, *The Complete Peterkin Papers*, 1960

782. The [newspaper] writer is speaking to a broad coalition of readers, and if he wants to be understood by most of them, he will write as plainly as possible. This is not the worst discipline for a writer.
—PETE HAMILL, Preface to *The Invisible City*, March 24, 1980

783. I may write again to-day, or at any moment, as things come into my head.
—THOMAS HARDY, letter to Emma Hardy, April 24, 1895

784. The brightest genius seldom puts the best of his own soul into his printed page; and some famous men have certainly put the worst of theirs.
—FREDRIC HARRISON, *The Choice of Books*, 1907

785. Moonlight, in a familiar room, falling so white upon the carpet, and showing all its figures so distinctly . . . is a medium the most suitable for a romance-writer to get acquainted with his illusive guests. . . . With this scene before him, if a man, sitting all alone, cannot dream strange things, and make them look like truth, he need never try to write romances.
—NATHANIEL HAWTHORNE, *The Scarlet Letter*, 1850

786. It is better to be able neither to read nor write than to be able to do nothing else.
—WILLIAM HAZLITT, "On the Ignorance of the Learned," in *Table Talk*, 1821

787. If I gave up teaching, I would have no time at all for writing.
—JOSEPH HELLER, *Playboy*, June 1975

788. They also agreed that, with a woman who could be gained by writing, they had rather have any man in the world for a rival than the King.
— LORD JOHN HERVEY, about himself and Robert Walpole, concerning King George II, *Memoirs*, 1848

789. A chief pleasure which the author of novels and stories experiences is that of becoming acquainted with the characters he draws. . . . They are at first mere embryos, outlines of distant personalities. By and by, if they have any organic cohesion, they begin to assert themselves.
— OLIVER WENDELL HOLMES, *Over the Teacups*, 1890

790. I find the great charm of writing consists in its surprises.
— OLIVER WENDELL HOLMES, *Over the Teacups*, 1890

791. If you invent, see that your
Characters be congruent.
— HORACE, *The Art of Poetry*

792. Sound sense is the first principle and source of writing well.
— HORACE, *The Art of Poetry*

793. All ye that write, material select,
That suits your powers, and see you long reflect.
— HORACE, *The Art of Poetry*

794. I have just finished reading the revised version of *The Devils*. . . . Your revisions have deepened and enriched the play in an extraordinary way, and I feel that it has now become a fully integrated work of dramatic art. I am glad you brought in the marriage ceremony. It adds another dimension to Grandier's character. [Another addition] will be a good thing, I feel, to let the audience know that he has an intellectual justification for what he is doing as well as an emotional and spiritual motive. As it is, you merely mention a book on priestly celibacy and pass on.
— ALDOUS HUXLEY, letter to John Whiting, January 1, 1961

795. Writing means summoning oneself to court and playing the judge's part.
— HENRIK IBSEN, letter to Ludwig Passarge, June 16, 1880

796. Everything that I have written has the closest possible connection with what I have lived through inwardly.
— HENRIK IBSEN, letter to Heinrich Laube, February 18, 1880

797. I believe that the dramatic categories are elastic, and that they must accommodate themselves to the literary facts — not vice versa.
— HENRIK IBSEN, letter to Heinrich Laube, February 18, 1880

798. To care more about how a story is told than about what it tells is a sign of a literary vocation.
— EUGENE IONESCO, conversation with Claude Bonnefoy, 1966

799. I think that if I get into the habit of writing a bit about what happens, or rather doesn't happen, I may lose a little of the sense of loneliness and desolation which abides with me.
— ALICE JAMES, diary, May 31, 1889

800. The fox is the novelist's idea, and when he rides straight he rides, regardless of the danger, in whatever direction that animal takes.
— HENRY JAMES, *English Hours*, 1905

801. When I write other things, I find it almost impossible to write letters.
— WILLIAM JAMES, letter to Henry James, February 14, 1907

802. Story, the dictionary tells one, is a short form of the word history.
— RANDELL JARRELL, "Stories" in *The Anchor Book of Stories*, 1958

803. I will put my law within them, and I will write it upon their hearts.
— JEREMIAH 3:3

804. The sin of Judah is written with a pen of iron; with a point of diamond it is engraved.
— JEREMIAH 17:1

805. Here is my signature! Let the Almighty answer me! Oh, that I had the indictment written by my adversary.
— JOB 31:35

806. What I have written, I have written.
— JOHN 19:22

807. You tell me that the printer to whom you sent my story *Two Gallants* before you read it yourself refuses to print it and therefore you ask me either to suppress it or to modify it in such a way as to enable it to pass. I cannot see my way to do either of these things. I have written my book with considerable care, in spite of a hundred difficulties and in accordance with what I understand to be the classical tradition of my art. You must therefore allow me to say that your printer's opinion of it does not interest me in the least. . . . You cannot really expect me to mutilate my work.

—JAMES JOYCE, letters to Grant Richard,
April 26, 1906 and May 20, 1906

808. The quality that makes a bad novel somehow forgivable is a fervent belief in the story, no matter how misled or ill expressed it may be.

—NORA JOHNSON, *New York Times Book Review*,
September 9, 1990

809. To have perception at the pitch of passion. Was it not this that . . . so many writers . . . were to miss.

—ALFRED KAZIN, paraphrasing Henry James,
On Native Grounds, 1942

810. When the columns [about the Army during the Korean War] were published . . . enlistments in the new Army dropped to zero, the first time I changed the world with my writing.

—WILLIAM KENNEDY, "Why It Took So Long,"
New York Times Book Review, May 20, 1990

811. Spend 3 years on first full novel (1100-page *Town and City*) which was cut to 400 pages by Harcourt-Brace and thereby reduced from a mighty (over-long, windy, but sincere) black book of sorrows into a "salable" ordinary novel (Never again editorship for me.)

—JACK KEROUAC, *Heaven and Other Poems*, 1957

812. I have been writing my heart out all my life, but only getting a living out of it now.

—JACK KEROUAC, *Heaven and Other Poems*, 1957

813. Belief and Technique for Modern Prose
— Write what you want bottomless from bottom of mind
— Write in recollection and amazement for yourself
— Don't think of words when you stop but to see picture better.

—JACK KEROUAC, *Heaven and Other Poems*, 1958

814. Fuck it! I'm just going to sit down and tell the truth.
—JACK KEROUAC, quoted by John Clellon Holmes
in *Jack's book* by Lenore Kandel, 1978

815. You read Plato's *Apology* and are enchanted; how infinitely witty he is, how pointed every word, how absolutely right—alas! And we who are corrupted by the accursed nonsense that the great thing is to be an author, we are tempted to read him as though he were an author, a witty author who might carry off the palm in the newspapers— but he is playing for life and death.

My life shows something similar, in a smaller measure. For my personal existence is worth much more, it is much more exhausting than my writings.
—SØREN KIERKEGAARD, "The Last Years," *Journal 1853–1855*

816. On writing—a matter of exercise. If you work out with weights for 15 minutes a day over a course of ten years, you're gonna get muscles. If you write for an hour and a half a day for ten years you're gonna turn into a good writer. . . . In a way I'm in therapy every day. People pay $135 an hour to sit on a couch. I'm talking about the same fears and inadequacies in my writing. . . . I write for that buried child in us but I'm writing for the grown-up too. I want grown-ups to look at the child long enough to be able to give him up. The child should be buried.
—STEPHEN KING, *Time* magazine, October 6, 1986

817. If two men quarrel in print, they do not speak to each other, they speak at each other.
—CHARLES KINGSLEY, letter, December 1846

818. Mercifully, the mere act of writing was, and always has been, a physical pleasure to me. This made it easier to throw away anything that did not turn out well: and to practice, as it were scales. . . . [The Anglo-Indian tales] were originally much longer than when they appeared, but the shortening of them, first to my own fancy after rapturous re-readings, and next to the space available, taught me that a tale from which pieces have been raked out is like a fire that has been poked. One does not know that the operation has been performed, but everyone feels the affect. . . . In an auspicious hour, read your final draft and consider faithfully, every paragraph, sentence and word, blacking out where requisite. . . . At the end of that time, re-read and you shall find that it will bear a second shortening. Finally, read it aloud alone and at leisure.
—RUDYARD KIPLING, *Something of Myself*, 1937

819. The thing is, *A Separate Peace*, wrote itself. No book can have been easier to get down on paper.
— JOHN KNOWLES, "My Separate Peace," *Esquire*, March, 1985

820. I had just finished writing the first chapter of *The Gladiators* — it was actually chapter five, for I had started writing it in the middle.
— ARTHUR KOESTLER, *The Invisible Writing*, 1954

821. One of the great Russians — I think it was Turgenev — could only write with his feet in a bucket of hot water under his desk, facing the open window of his room. I believe that this position is typical for the novelist.
— ARTHUR KOESTLER, "The Novelist's Temptations," in *The Yogi and the Commissar*, 1945

822. By the pen, and what they write, you are not mad.
— THE KORAN, *The Pen*, 68:1

823. Writing a novel is very complicated. If I had to teach a class on writing a novel, I would suggest writing the major point for each chapter on a card. Then, hang them up in order and write in the details. Of course, I don't follow my own advice.
— MICHAEL KORDA, interview in *Dutchess Magazine*, Vol. 5, No. 4, Sept./Oct. 1990

824. My experience is that the test of a writer is the second book. If you don't get the second book out, the author disappears. Fiction writing should be constantly telling stories.
— MICHAEL KORDA, interview in *Dutchess Magazine*, Vol. 5, No. 4, Sept./Oct. 1990

825. The same common sense which makes an author write good things, makes him dread they are not good enough to deserve reading.
— LA BRUYÈRE, *Characters*, 1688

826. I don't know why I write, except from the propensity misery has to tell her griefs.
— CHARLES LAMB, letter to Coleridge, May 12, 1800

827. When my sonnet was rejected, I exclaimed, "Damn the age: I will write for antiquity."
— CHARLES LAMB, letter to Bryan Waller Procter, January 22, 1829

828. Often I am asked if any writer ever helped or advised me. None did. However, I was not asking for help either, and I do not believe one should. If one wishes to write, he or she had better be writing, and there is no real way in which one writer can help another. Each must find his own way.

—LOUIS L'AMOUR, *Education of a Wandering Man*, 1986

829. It is words and their associations which are untranslatable, not ideas; there is no idea, whether originating in a Hebrew, Greek or other mind, which cannot be adequately produced as an idea in English words; the reason why Shakespeare and Dante are practically untranslatable is that, recognizing how every word means more than itself to its native users.

—SIDNEY LANIER, Lecture XII, March 26, 1881

830. Nostalgia reveals itself in writing—or hides itself—in a number of ways, and it lives just as contentedly within works of "quality" or "excellence" as it does within those of mediocrity or even outright trashiness. In the latter—in the so-called "genre" romances, for example—anybody can see it, since it tends to be obvious, superficial and transparent. In "serious" writing, though, it can be a more elusive quality, partly because all aspects of serious writing, including the use of the past, tend, obviously, to be more refined, subtle, and complex.

Even so, it can be said in general that nostalgia in serious writing is betokened by one kind or other of aesthetic or emotional conservatism, whether in form, tone, subject matter, or attitude.... Turning to the past, of course, can be done in differing degrees and manners, with differing purposes and with differing degrees of success. But the using of the past is one thing, while a nostalgic falling into the past is clearly another; and it seems indisputable, if nothing else, that just now, a strong nostalgia impulse plays an important part in much of our current and most praised writing.

—ERIC LARSEN, "Writing and Nostalgia: Hiding in Past"
in *Writing in the Nuclear Age*, 1984

831. To this day, I still have the uneasy haunted feeling, and would rather not write most of the things I do write—including this note.

—D. H. LAWRENCE, "Phoenix," posthumous paper, 1936

832. Melville is a master of violent, chaotic physical motion, he can keep up a whole wild chase without a flaw. He is as perfect at creating stillness.

—D. H. LAWRENCE, *The Symbolic Meaning*, 1923

833. Contrary to what many of you might imagine, a career in letters is not without its drawbacks — chief among them the unpleasant fact that one is frequently called upon to actually sit down and write.
— FRAN LEBOWITZ, *Metropolitan Life*, 1974–1978

834. You can't write. You call another writer. He can't write either. This is terrific. You can now talk about not writing for 2 hours.
— FRAN LEBOWITZ, *Metropolitan Life*, 1974–1978

835. This is a book I wish I had written.
— ERICH LEINSDORF, about Robert Donington's *Opera and Its Symbols, New York Times*, January 13, 1991

836. To portray the collective mood and the mass culture requires technical innovation in the novel.
— MAX LERNER, "The America of John Dos Passos" in *Nation* 143, August 15, 1936

837. Most good writing today has overtones of symbolism.
— MAX LERNER, *Ideas for the Ice Age*, 1941

838. For there is never anywhere to go but in.
— DORIS LESSING, epigraph for *Briefing for a Descent into Hell*, 1971

839. I must unroll my book again. It would be better to rewrite it from the beginning, but I think there's no time for that. . . . Since I cannot mend the book, I must add to it. To leave it as it was would be to die perjured; I know so much more than I did about the woman who wrote it. What began the change was the very writing itself. Let no one lightly set about such a work. Memory, once waked, will play the tyrant.
— C. S. LEWIS, *Till We Have Faces*, 1956

840. In writing narrative . . . you keep close all the time to everyday speech . . . in dialogue you reproduce it . . . as if you were writing for the stage.
— WYNDHAM LEWIS, letter to David Kahma, January 30, 1948

841. When he can read English well, it will be seasonable to enter him in writing: And here the first thing should be taught him is, to hold his pen right.
— JOHN LOCKE, *Some Thoughts Concerning Education*, 1705

842. But as I went on writing and simultaneously talking with other women, young and old, with different lives and experiences — those who supported themselves, those who wished careers, those who were hard-working housewives and mothers, and those with more ease — I found that my point of view was not unique.

. . . Gradually, these chapters, fed by conversations, arguments, and revelations from men and women of all groups, became more than my individual story, until I decided in the end to give back to the people who had shared and stimulated many of these thoughts.

— ANNE MORROW LINDBERGH, *Gift from the Sea*, 1955

843. Nothing was heard in the room but the hurrying pen of the stripling, busily writing epistles important.

— HENRY WADSWORTH LONGFELLOW, *The Courtship of Miles Standish*, I, 81, 1858

844. It should be self-evident that a man who wants to write well must learn his craft from other writers. He should read, read, read. All the time he is absorbing unconsciously the art of writing.

— ROGER SHERMAN LOOMIS, *The Art of Writing Prose*, 1930

845. Crabbe wrote far too much . . . and rewrote far too little.

— F. L. LOOMIS, on George Crabbe in the Introduction to *George Crabbe, An Anthology*, 1933

846. When poets first began
      To tell men's deeds in song; nor long before
      Were letters first devised.

— LUCRETIUS, *On the Nature of Things*, Book V, lines 1438–1440

847. I have not sought to adorn my work with long phrases or high-sounding words or any of those superficial attractions and ornaments with which many writers seek to embellish their material.

— NICCOLÒ MACHIAVELLI, *The Prince*, 1512

848. Your suggestion that I do critical work to get into step with myself is a very keen bit of analysis. I have a perfectly clear cut dissatisfaction with what I have already done but no more than a sort of sense of gravitation toward the thing that would give me satisfaction to do. Of course I have been trying to get my ideas into shape but they remain pretty nebulous so far. The rhythmic problem troubles me for one thing. . . . I find that under the pressure of any sort of emotion I fall back into cadences which I know to be stale before I use them. Working

with deliberation I can get effects that don't disgust me on rereading but
only then. That's one thing. The other is the equally basic problem of
verbiage. What are the living waters of the world? As I tried to say before I don't think Miss [Marianne] Moore's attempt to give poetic edge
to words already stale in academic or commercial conversation gets by.
Neither do I feel that the extensive use of words generally omitted from
polite conversation is enough, though one must admit that it appears to
give reality. Neither again does it seem enough to twist the order of
words *inter sese* for the purpose of directing attention. The dodge is too
obvious.
    —ARCHIBALD MacLEISH, letter to Amy Lowell, March 3, 1924

849. I can't think of a thing to write. It could be another case of
writer's block . . . but most likely it's a much more widespread affliction
. . . brain cramp.
    —PERFESSER, from the comic strip *Shoe* by Jeff MacNelly,
                        in *Shake the Hand, Bite the Taco*, 1986

850. Style, of course, is what every good young author looks to acquire. In lovemaking it is equivalent to grace. Everybody wants it but
nobody seems to find it by working directly toward the goal. On the
other hand, unless born with style or grace, nobody seems to get there
without working hard in some direction or other. . . . The *Naked and the
Dead* had been written out of what I could learn from James T. Farrell
and John Dos Passos with good doses of Thomas Wolfe and Tolstoy. . . .
With all such help, it was a book that wrote itself. It had a style-proof
style. That is to say it had a best-seller style, no style. . . . I knew however it was no literary achievement. I had done a book in a general style
borrowed from many people and did not know what I had of my own
to say. I had not had enough of my own life yet. The idea could even
be advanced that style comes to young authors about the time they
recognize that life is out there ready to kill them, kill them quickly or
slowly, but something out there is not fooling.
    —NORMAN MAILER, *Advertisement for Myself*, 1959

851. When I write about ducks I swear that I am a white duck with
a round eye, floating in a pond fringed with yellow blobs and taking an
occasional dart at the other duck with the round eye, which floats up-
side down beneath me. In fact this whole process of becoming the duck
(what Lawrence would, perhaps, call this "consummation with the duck
or the apple") is so thrilling that I can hardly breathe, only to think about
it. For although that is as far as most people can get, it is really only the
"prelude." There follows the moment when you are more duck, more

apple, or more Natasha then any of these objects could ever possibly be, and so you create them anew ... I believe in technique ... because I don't see how art is going to make that divine spring into the bounding outline of things if it hasn't passed through the process of trying to become these things before recreating them.

—KATHERINE MANSFIELD, letter to Dorothy Best,
October 11, 1917

852. For this year I have two wishes: to write, to make money.

—KATHERINE MANSFIELD, *Journal*, January 1, 1915

853. From a writer's standpoint it takes a vast number of disconnected memories and impressions to create a satisfactory illusion of reality.

—JOHN MARQUAND, *Esquire*, 1940

854. At the end of a half a volume, I became aware that it was excessively dull, and I stopped. Many years afterwards I burned it.

—HARRIET MARTINEAU, *Autobiography*, 1821

855. Some of your people, notably Dot and the mother, haunt the mind as presences long after one has read or seen the play.

—JOHN MASEFIELD, letter to John Galsworthy
about his play, *The Eldest Son*, November 12, 1912

856. Nothing is so unsafe as to put into a novel a person drawn line by line from life.... Strangely enough, he does not make the other characters of the book seem false, but himself.

—W. SOMERSET MAUGHAM, *Six Stories Written
in the First Person Singular*, 1931

857. When I have finished this book, I shall know where I stand.

—W. SOMERSET MAUGHAM, *The Summing Up*, 1948

858. Fiction is stranger than fact.

—W. SOMERSET MAUGHAM, *Opium Den,
On a Chinese Screen*, 1922

859. A real writer never has any hint of whether his book will be born as a river, stream, or brook.

—FRANÇOIS MAURIAC, *Second Thoughts*, 1961

860. To write is to give oneself away.

—FRANÇOIS MAURIAC, *God and Man*, 1929

861. The margins [of the unfinished novel *Sténie*] are filled with his self-reproaching comments: To be done again . . . to be corrected.
— ANDRÉ MAUROIS, on Balzac in *Prometheus*, 1965

862. Despite the existence of several thousand creative writing programs around the country, there is probably no good answer to the question of whether writing can be taught.
— JAN MCINERNEY, "Raymond Carver: A Small Still Voice,"
New York Times, August 6, 1989

863. Mr. Vonnegut is still asking the big, embarrassing, childish teleological questions. He is probably our leading literary big-question maker. He keeps posing the kinds of questions, as he himself once put it, that college sophomores ask.
— JAY MCINERNEY, *New York Times*
Book Review, September 9, 1990

864. Everybody is always quoting the very last paragraph, about the snow falling softly through the universe. Maybe instead of writing this story, Joyce should simply have written a poem about snow falling through the universe.
— THOMAS MERTON, about James Joyce's "The Dead"
from *Dubliners* in *The Secular Journal*, June 1, 1941

865. I guess if you read novels, you may be a real novelist. I can't read novels anymore. That's why I am writing a journal.
— THOMAS MERTON, *The Secular Journal*, May 19, 1941

866. Why are you making your will as a writer already? Impatience. Go on, fool! Forget it! You may well write another twenty books, who knows? But what does it matter. It is not the writing that matters, or the books either, or who reads them.
That is just the point. This idea of a "writing career" which begins somewhere and ends somewhere is also a beautifully stupid fiction . . . I don't feel that my days as a writer are over. I don't care where they are . . . . It is time to give to others whatever I have to give and not reflect on it. I wish I had learned the knack of doing this without question or care.
— THOMAS MERTON, *Conjectures of a Guilty Bystander*, 1965

867. My spare time was devoted to a complete re-writing of the book from its commencement. It is in this way that all my books have been composed. They were always written at least twice over; a first

draft of the entire work was completed to the very end of the subject, then the whole begun again *de novo*.
—JOHN STUART MILL, *Autobiography*, 1873

868. [Rationale of Judicial Evidence] . . . was itself no small acquisition. But this occupation did for me what might seem less to be expected; it gave a great start to my powers of composition. Everything which I wrote subsequently . . . was markedly superior to anything that I had written before it. . . . I added to it by the assiduous reading of other writers . . . Goldsmith, Fielding, Pascal, Voltaire, and Courier. Through these influences my writing lost the jejuneness of my early compositions; the bones and cartilages began to clothe themselves with flesh, and the style became, at times, lively and almost light.
—JOHN STUART MILL, *Autobiography*, 1873

869. You feared I might be ill. I am far worse than ill. My husband has died. I cannot write about it, nor about anything else.
—EDNA ST. VINCENT MILLAY, letter to
Manuel Mischoulon, December 10, 1949

870. It is a story and it has a real hero, and a real heroine, and a plot, and its characters are, of course, just the people you and I have known all our lives.
—EDNA ST. VINCENT MILLAY, letter to
Horace Liveright, November 1922

871. Questioner: Are any of your plays about your own life?
Arthur Miller: Not really but I'm in all the plays.
—ARTHUR MILLER, *New York Times*, March 10, 1991

872. When it comes to writing I think my talent has always been fundamentally and essentially for the drama. I've never been comfortable writing in any other way. I know I can do in three pages of dialogue what would take me endless pages of words.
—ARTHUR MILLER, attributed by Josh Greenfield,
New York Times, February 13, 1972

873. The question of freedom, the privilege to put down my thoughts somewhere and not permit anyone to pry into them.
—HENRY MILLER, letter to Anaïs Nin, April 10, 1932

874. The impulse to put everything down immediately is a weakness—a neurotic fear of losing something. You should know by now that

the memory is an immense steel reservoir—nothing escapes it. Write immediately, yes! But as an artist.
— HENRY MILLER, letter to Anaïs Nin, October 12, 1933

875. A work of literature is the act whereby a mind takes possession of space, time, nature, or other minds.
— J. HILLIS MILLER, *The Disappearance of God*, 1963

876. As Brother Francis readily admitted, his mastery of pre-Deluge English was far from masterful yet. The way nouns could sometimes modify nouns in that tongue had always been one of his weak points.
— WALTER M. MILLER, JR., *A Canticle for Leibowitz*, 1960

877. Yiddish seethed with living idiom and abounded with the warmth and elasticity so congenial to the creation of readable fiction. Faced with the problem of creating dialogue, for instance, Hebrew novelists were at their wits' end.
— DAN MIRON, *A Traveler Disguised*, 1973

878. When I first started writing, I used to write more fictionally. . . . Like any fiction writer there was some basis in something that happened. . . . To be a great actor you would have to have felt what the character felt and be able to draw it out. It's the same in writing.
— JONI MITCHELL, *Written in My Soul*, 1986

879. Sherwood Anderson regularly wrote in the morning and spent the afternoon in other pursuits—a routine that led the young William Faulkner in New Orleans to exclaim, "If this is what it takes to be a novelist, then that's the life for me."
— CHARLES E. MODLIN, in "Sherwood Anderson: An Appreciation," *Atlantic Monthly* 191 (June 1953)

880. The art of measuring brings the world into subjection to man; the art of writing prevents his knowledge from perishing along with himself; together they make man.
— THEODORE MOMMSEN, *The History of Rome*, 1854

881. With what heart can people write, when they believe their letters will never be received?
— (LADY) MARY WORTLEY MONTAGU, letter to Anne Wortley, August 8, 1709

882. Reading stories is bad enough but writing them is worse.
— LUCY MAUD MONTGOMERY, *Anne of Green Gables*, 1908

883. It's a sad sweet story. I just cried like a child while I was writing it.
— LUCY MAUD MONTGOMERY, *Anne of Green Gables*, 1908

884. Writing is exciting
and baseball is like writing.
You can never tell with either
how far it will go
or what you will do
— MARIANNE MOORE, *The Complete Poems of. . .*, 1967

885. If I would with my writing declare how much pleasure and comfort your daughterly loving letters were unto me, a peck of coals would not suffice to make me the pen.
— SIR THOMAS MORE, letter to his daughter, Margaret Roper, Tower of London, 1534

886. Even as a child I was writing. I wrote through high school and college and babies and just kept writing. When the children were very young, poetry was the most I could grab time for.
— MARY MCGARRY MORRIS, *Publishers Weekly*, December 7, 1990

887. My style of writing is organic. I go from one page to the next page, and I read on the page how well or how poorly I am doing. I take my clues, in the main, from what I have done. I feel my way toward the book's form.
— WRIGHT MORRIS, conversation with Wayne C. Booth, 1975

888. He writes very noisily and briefly; any competent writer could have knocked off the text of the *Medium Is the Message* in an afternoon.
— MALCOLM MUGGERIDGE, on McLuhan in *Esquire*, August 1967

889. Hardy takes a short cut to tragedy by reducing life to a formula. He gets rid beforehand of the main obstacle to tragedy, which is man's natural inclination to avoid it.
— EDWIN MUIR, *Essays on Literature and Society*, 1965

890. From my earliest years I have delighted in verse and I have occupied myself — and sometimes allayed my griefs, which have been

no more, I know, than any sojourner on earth must encounter—with many floundering efforts at its composition. My fingers, indeed, were always too clumsy for crochetwork, and those dazzling productions of embroidery which one sees often—the overflowing fruit and flower baskets, the little Dutch boys, the bonneted maidens with their watering can—have likewise proved to be beyond my skill. So I offer instead, as a product of my leisure hours, these rude poises, these ballads, couplets, reflections.
—ALICE MUNRO, "Meneseteung," *The New Yorker*, January 11, 1988

891. This wish-to-write is very common. It is often vague, intermittent, a mere emotional itch, a weak yen, a daydream. It can be easily fobbed off. It can be quickly exhausted by a few hours of typing. Often, it is like a paper fire, a bright blaze soon over.
—GORHAM MUNSON, *The Written Word*, 1949

892. All I know is that at a very early stage of the novel's development I get this urge to collect bits of straw and fluff, and to eat pebbles.
—VLADIMIR NABOKOV, *Playboy*, January 1964

893. Of all the definitions mouthed by a certain branch of the critical fraternity, that which has to do with creation in literary fields is the most completely bogus.
—G. J. NATHAN, *Testament of a Critic*, 1931

894. The Viennese writes of love at 5 P.M. The Frenchman, of love at 12:30 A.M.
—G. J. NATHAN, *The World in Falseface*, 1923

895. One of the fallacies that hovers over the literary art is that the writer who thinks clearly will pretty generally write clearly. . . . The fallacy of the short sentence as a symbol of clear and direct thought is equally persistent.
—G. J. NATHAN, *American Mercury*, June 1929

896. It takes a lover to write a novel of love, even before it takes a writer.
—G. J. NATHAN, *Monks Are Monks*, 1929

897. The object which led to my writing at all, has also led me, in writing, to turn my thoughts in a different direction.
—JOHN HENRY NEWMAN, "Apologia Pro Vita Sua," January 31, 1864

898. Every novel must do one of three things—it must (1) tell something, (2) show something or (3) prove something. Some novels do all three of these; some do only two; all must do at least one.
—FRANK NORRIS, "The True Reward of the Novelist,"
World's Work, October 1901

899. Things can happen in some cities and the tale of them will be interesting; the same story laid in another city would be ridiculous.
—FRANK NORRIS, "An Opening for Novelists"
in *The Wave*, May 22, 1897

900. The complications of real life are infinitely better, stronger and more original than anything you can make up. The only difference is in the matter of selection of details.
—FRANK NORRIS, "Fiction Is Selection" in *The Wave*,
September 11, 1897

901. Writing fiction today [1970] sometimes seems an exercise in stubbornness and an anachronistic gesture that goes against the shrill tenets of the age—that only the present has meaning, that the contemplative life is irrelevant, that only the life of purest sensation is divine and that the act of giving shape to sensation, of giving a permanence to the present, is somehow an inversion of the life principle itself. But writers of prose are tough, meticulous people, dedicated to a systematic analysis of the life of sensation and of the electronic paradise that threatens to make language itself obsolete. Writers of prose are all historians, dealing with the past. It is the legendary quality of the past we are most interested in, the immediate past, mysterious and profound, that feeds into the future. It's writers who create history.
—JOYCE CAROL OATES, remarks at National Book Awards, 1970,
quoted in the *New York Times Book Review*, November 16, 1986

902. There is in the short story at its most characteristic something we do not often find in the novel—an intense awareness of human loneliness.
—FRANK O'CONNER, *The Lonely Voice*, 1962

903. Names of characters . . . right names always tough job.
—EUGENE O'NEILL, *New York Herald Tribune*,
November 3, 1931

904. I did nothing today except write.
—JOE ORTON, diary, December 21, 1966

905. I shall write better, but never, I think, so well as I talk; for then I feel inspired. The means are pleasant; my voice excites me, my pen never.
— MARGARET FULLER (OSSOLI), *Memoirs*, 1884

906. Much did I write, but what I thought defective I gave in person to the flames for their revision. Even when I was setting forth into exile I burned certain verse.
— OVID, *Tristia*, Book IV, 10, lines 61–63

907. Grant indulgence to my writings, for their purpose has been not my renown but my advantage, and to do homage to others.
— OVID, *Epistulae, Ex Ponto*, Book III, 9

908. While writing the very toil gives pleasure and itself is lessened, and the growing work glows along with the writer's heart.
— OVID, *Epistulae, Ex Ponto*, Book III, 9

909. One argued that the manuscript could not be authentic. It lacked spirit.
— ERIC PANKEY, "Apocrypha," *The Quarterly*, Fall, 1989, No. 11

910. If, with the literate, I am
Impelled to try an epigram
I never seek to take the credit;
We all assume that Oscar said it.
— DOROTHY PARKER, *Not So Deep as a Well*, 1936

911. The present letter is a very long one, simply because I had no leisure to make it shorter.
— BLAISE PASCAL, *Lettres Provinciales* XVI, 1656

912. The essence of all good style, whatever its accidents may be, is expressiveness. It is mastered in proportion to the justice, the nicety with which words balance or match their meaning, and their writer succeeds in saying what he wills.
— WALTER PATER, on Pascal,
Contemporary Review, December 1894

913. Somebody compared novel-writing to having a baby, but for me it is the conception which is painful and the delivery which is easy.
— WALKER PERCY, *Shenandoah* 18, Spring 1967

914. When I've thought over what I wish to say, it is not so well said as when I write and think at the same time, though the mechanical part of the premeditated letter is better.

—BLISS PERRY, quoting Henry Lee Higginson, 1921

915. No one writes, even in a short story, as well as he ought. He is fortunate if he has written as well as he could.

—BLISS PERRY, *Bedside Book of Famous British Stories*, 1940

916. Rattling good stories . . . contain characters so filled with the breath of life that a reader can no more forget them than he could forget his most intimate friend.

—WILLIAM LYON PHELPS, *The Advance of the English Novel*, 1927

917. If I were born Chinese I would not be a painter but a writer. I'd write my pictures.

—PABLO PICASSO, circa 1956, quoted by Dore Ashton in *Picasso on Art*, 1972

918. It's very easy to write when you're a writer; you have the words trained and they come to your hand like birds.

—PABLO PICASSO, in *La Publicitat*, October 19, 1926, quoted by Dore Ashton in *Picasso on Art*, 1972

919. Character is at the heart of a story.

—BELVA PLAIN, *New York Times Book Review*, May 6, 1990

920. Some things are hard to write about. After something happens to you, you go to write it down, and either you overdramatize it or underplay it, exaggerate the wrong parts or ignore the important ones. At any rate, you never write it quite the way you want to.

—SYLVIA PLATH, *Journal*, July 1950

921. I extremely approve of your care in revising your works; remember, however, this exactness has its limits: too much polishing rather weakens than strengths a performance.

—PLINY, *Letters*, Book IX, 35

922. Charles Dickens, in a note lying before me, alluding to an examination I once made of the mechanism of "Barnaby Rudge," says— "By the way, are you aware that Godwin wrote his 'Caleb Williams' backwards? He first involved his hero in a web of difficulties, forming the

second volume, and then, for the first, cast him about for some mode of accounting for what had been done."
— EDGAR ALLAN POE, "The Philosophy of Composition," *Graham's Magazine*, April 1846

923. True ease in writing comes from Art, not chance
As those move easiest who have learned to dance.
— ALEXANDER POPE, *The Dunciad*, Book II, 362–363, 1728

924. Some judge of Author's Names, not works
And then, nor praise nor blame
The Writings, but the Men.
— ALEXANDER POPE, *The Dunciad*, Book II, 412–413, 1728

925. For thee we dim the eyes, and stuff the head
With all such reading as was never read;
For thee explain a thing till all men doubt it,
And write about it.
— ALEXANDER POPE, *The Dunciad*, Book IV, 248–252, 1728

926. It is an old saying that every human being possesses in his own life and experience the material for one novel.
— KATHERINE ANNE PORTER, *My First Speech*, Paris, 1934

927. A writer may be inspired occasionally: That's his good luck; but he doesn't learn to write by inspiration: he works at it.
— KATHERINE ANNE PORTER, *My First Speech*, Paris, 1934

928. Just in proportion as the writer's aim, consciously or unconsciously, comes to be the transcribing, not of the world, not of mere fact, but of his sense of it, he becomes an artist, his work a fine art, and good art in proportion to the truth of his presentment of that sense.
— LELAND POWERS, *Practice Book*, 1916, attributed to Lucius P. Monroe, *The Sixth Sense*

929. Always in doubt about his characters, subject to all the waverings of sensibility, running round to his friends for advice because he had no confidence in his own judgment, Turgenev managed, at least, and like a naturalist, to pin his hero to the paper.
— V. S. PRITCHETT, *In My Good Books*, 1942

930. If he knew how to write novels he did not know how to write

plays . . . his passion for detail, his endless dialogue got in the way. He was a born explainer and lacked the gift of omission.

— V. S. PRITCHETT, on Balzac in *Balzac*, 1973

931. Have I not written to you thirty sayings of admonition and knowledge.

— PROVERBS 22:20

932. My tongue is the pen of a ready writer.

— PSALMS 45:1

933. To write jargon is to be perpetually shuffling around in the fog.

— SIR ARTHUR QUILLER-COUCH, *On the Art of Writing*, 1916

934. Whenever in your reading you come across one of these words, case, instance, character, nature, condition, persuasion, degree — whenever in writing your pen betrays you to one or another of them — pull yourself up and take thought.

— SIR ARTHUR QUILLER-COUCH, "On Jargon"
from *On the Art of Writing*, 1916

935. Writing is of the utmost importance . . . but a sluggish pen delays our thoughts.

— QUINTILIAN, Book I, i, 28

936. I was aware acutely, and in a way that makes writing impossible, of the existence of language as mere symbol.

— DAVID RABE, Introduction to
The Basic Training of Pavlo Hummel, 1973

937. Lamb almost raised the pun to a higher power. His puns very often mean something. A pun is like one of those scientific toys that rotate in a vacuum: he almost made it do work.

— SIR WALTER ALEXANDER RALEIGH,
On Writing and Writers, 1926

938. Literature does not have the power of creating emotion out of something that contains none.

— JULES RENARD, "Diary," October 1903

939. You can recover from the writing malady only by falling mortally ill and dying.

— JULES RENARD, "Diary," February 1895

940. Yes, the story I am writing exists, written in absolutely perfect fashion, some place, in the air. All I must do is find it, and copy it.
— JULES RENARD, "Diary," February 1895

941. Writing for someone is like writing to someone: you immediately feel obliged to lie.
— JULES RENARD, "Diary," January 1908

942. To write, constantly to write! But nature does not constantly produce. She gives flowers and fruits in her season, and then she rests for at least six months. Which is about my measure.
— JULES RENARD, "Diary," March 1908

943. There is no form of writing in which the fluid idiom of the language can be seen to better effect in its changes and in its movements.
— ERNEST RHYS, Introduction to
A Century of English Essays, 1913

944. I think what's important is that you write what's really, really intense, and what gives you the greatest thrill.
— ANN RICE, quoted in
New York Times Magazine, October 14, 1990

945. To believe that the novelist has "something to say" and that he then looks for a way to say it represents the gravest of misconceptions.
— ALAIN ROBBE-GRILLET, *For a New Novel*, 1965

946. Beware of cleverness; think of nothing but greatness. Make up your mind to write the greatest short stories in the world, and do not permit yourself even to dream that you cannot write them.
— EDWIN ARLINGTON ROBINSON, letter to
Edith Brower, March 14, 1897

947. Writing even a six-line trade-paper advertisement cost me intolerable effort. My brain wouldn't function. My fingers were paralyzed. I was fighting the cold wind of absurdity blowing off the waste lands of our American commercial chaos.
— JAMES RORTY, *I Was an Ad-Man Once*, 1934

948. The real object of my Confessions is, to contribute to an accurate knowledge of my inner being in all the different situations of my life. What I have promised to relate, is the history of my soul; I need

no other memories in order to write it faithfully; it is sufficient for me
to enter again into my inner self as I have hitherto done.
— JEAN-JACQUES ROUSSEAU, *The Confessions*, 1766

949. Anybody can tell stories. . . . Liars and cheats, and crooks, for
example. But for stories with that Extra Ingredient, ah, for those, even
the best storytellers need the Story Waters. Storytelling needs fuel.
— SALMAN RUSHDIE, *Haroun and the Sea of Stories*, 1990

950. Literature meant telling—telling fine tales. Why were they
fine? Because they were well worked out. There was a beginning and
an end and inside there were characters.
— JEAN-PAUL SARTRE, to Simone De Beauvoir, *Adieux*, 1981

951. At first glance, it would appear that surgery and writings have
little in common, but I think that it is not so. For one thing, they are
both sub-celestial arts; as far as I know, the angels disdain to perform
either one. In each of them you hold a slender instrument that leaves
a trail whenever it is applied. In one, there is the shedding of blood; in
the other is ink that is spilled upon the page. In one, the scalpel is
restrained; in the other, the pen is given rein. The surgeon sutures together the tissues of the body to make whole what is sick or injured; the
writer sews words into sentences to fashion a new version of human
experience. A surgical operation is rather like a short story. You make
the incision, rummage around inside a bit, then stitch up. It has a beginning, a middle and an end. If I were to choose a medical specialist to
write a novel it would be a psychiatrist. They tend to go on and on. And
on.
— RICHARD SELZER, "The Pen and the Scalpel,"
New York Times Magazine, August 21, 1988

952. Last November I was fourteen, and Papa gave me this lovely
diary for my birthday. It's a shame to spoil these beautiful white pages
with writing.
— ANNEMARIE SELINKO, *Désirée*, 1953

953. I suppose my head has always been full of images.
— PETER SHAFFER, a note on the book *Equus*, 1974

954. Who fears a sentence or an old man's saw
Shall by a painted cloth be kept in awe.
— SHAKESPEARE, *The Rape of Lucrece*, 1594

955. Write till your ink be dry; and with
your tears moist it again; and
frame some feeling line that may
discover such integrity.
— SHAKESPEARE, *Two Gentlemen of Verona*, III, ii

956. Why is my verse so barren of new pride?
So far from variations or quick change?
— SHAKESPEARE, Sonnet 76, 1-2

957. I do love and it hath taught me to rhyme.
— SHAKESPEARE, *Love's Labour's Lost*, IV, iii

958. Assist me, some extemporal god of rhyme,
For I am sure I shall turn sonneteer,
Devise, wit; write, pen; for I am
For whole volumes in folio.
— SHAKESPEARE, *Love's Labour's Lost*, I, ii

959. I sat me down, densed a new commission;
Wrote it fair; I once did hold it,
As our statists do, a baseness to write fair
And labored much how to forget that learning.
— SHAKESPEARE, *Hamlet*, V, ii

960. I have never admitted the right of an elderly author to alter the work of a young author, even when the young author happens to be his former self.
— GEORGE BERNARD SHAW, *The Quintessence of Ibsenism*, 1913

961. Almost everything has been reversed, sometimes radically, but often merely to eliminate references to time ("yesterday," "last week") or place. May the reader be duped into thinking that truth is omnipresent and eternal.
— ISRAEL SHENKER, Preface to *Words and Their Masters*, 1974

962. You write with ease, to show your breeding
But easy writing's vile hard reading.
— RICHARD SHERIDAN, *Clio's Protest*, 1771

963. The prose seems utterly with artifice, the people exhibit the most elemental feelings, but it soon becomes clear that the book deals with the reality that lies below the surface of the world.
— EARL SHORRIS, on Tomás Rivera's *And the Earth Did Not Devour Him*, in *New York Times Book Review*, July 15, 1990

964. Consider, moreover, how children learned to write, a skill on the endangered species list in contemporary education.
— JOHN SILBER, on teaching handwriting, speech, May 17, 1981

965. One little girl has to ask to spell every word she wants to use, but her inability to spell does not daunt her in the least; she keeps writing and writing and writing.
— CHARLES SILBERMAN, *Crisis in the Classroom*, 1970

966. When John [Berryman] congratulated him on the prize, and added, "High time!" Eliot said, "Rather too soon. The Nobel is a ticket to one's own funeral. No one has ever done anything after he got it." John protested: it was not so. "All of Yeats' great poetry was written after he received the award."
— EILEEN SIMPSON, *Poets in Their Youth: A Memoir*, 1982

967. For of all love stories in the world, the deepest and most cutting ones are the stories of parents and children. Or as my father once said to me, "It's not easy being King Lear."
— BRETT SINGER, "Bloodlines," *Esquire*, February 1985

968. The problem was that in order to write with skill about people of the world, one needed to know the world. . . . I only knew Jews that spoke Yiddish. Even then I knew a writer can only write about people and things he knows well.
— ISAAC BASHEVIS SINGER, *A Young Man in Search of Love*, 1978

969. I can't write prose excepting when I am writing about poetry.
— EDITH SITWELL, letter to John Lehmann, May 21, 1951

970. The essay writer is a chartered libertine, and a law unto himself. A quick ear and eye, an ability to discern the infinite suggestiveness of common things, a broadening meditative spirit, are all the essayist requires to start business with.
— ALEXANDER SMITH, "On the Writing of Essays" from *Dreamthorp*, 1863

971. In my later years I have sought to become simpler, straighter, and purer in my handling of the language. I've had many writing heros, writers who have influenced me. Of the ones still alive, I can think of E. B. White. I certainly admire the pure, crystal stream of his prose. When I was very young as a sportswriter I knowingly and unashamedly imitated others. I had a series of heros who would delight me for a while

... Damon Runyon, Westbrook Pigler, Joe Williams [who] at the top of his game ... was pretty good.
I think you pick up something from this guy and something from that.... I deliberately imitated those three guys, one by one, never together. I'd read one daily, faithfully, and be delighted by him and imitate him. Then someone else would catch my fancy. That's a shameful admission. But slowly, by what process I have no idea, your own writing tends to crystalize, to take shape. Yet you have learned some moves from all these guys and they are somehow incorporated into your style. Pretty soon you're not imitating any longer.
— RED SMITH, *No Cheering in the Press Box*, 1973

972. I am very glad that a lot of people in the West read what I write. But my main readership is, of course, in my own country, and it is for them that I am writing.
— ALEKSANDR SOLZHENITSYN, interview with Janis Sapiets, 1979

973. I am going to keep a journal because I cannot accept the fact that I feel so shattered that I cannot write at all ... the best thing is to write anything, anything at all that comes into your head, until gradually there is a calm and creative day.
— STEPHEN SPENDER, *Journal*, September 3, 1939

974. I am not breaking my head over the writing of my "little life." It is like fishing with a line; I write whatever comes to the end of my pen.
— ST. THERESA OF LISIEUX, Fall 1897, attributed by John Clarke in his translation of *Story of My Soul*

975. After my death, you must not speak to anyone about my manuscript before it is published.
— ST. THERESA OF LISIEUX, August 1, 1897, attributed by John Clarke in his translation of *Story of My Soul*

976. Let blockheads read what blockheads write.
— PHILIP STANHOPE, letter, November 1, 1750

977. "I was about 25 when I wrote this," he said, pointing to "Sense of Humor," the first of his stories published. He had trouble with it, he recalled, because he wanted to portray his protagonist as a dull man. Instead, he wrote a dull story.
— DEBORAH STEAD, about V. S. Pritchett, *New York Times*, March 24, 1991

978. You never took writing to mean self-expression, which means self-indulgence. You understood from the beginning that writing is done with words and sentences, and you spent hundreds of hours educating your ear, writing and rewriting and rewriting until you began to handle words in combination as naturally as one changes tones with the tongue and lips in whistling.
— WALLACE STEGNER, "To a Young Writer" in
One Way to Spell Man, 1982

979. What is a sentence. A sentence is an imagined master piece.
— GERTRUDE STEIN, *How to Write,* 1973

980. Editor: The reader won't understand. What you call counterpoint only slows the book.
   Writer: It has to be slowed — else how would you know when it goes fast.
— JOHN STEINBECK, *Journal of a Novel/
The East of Eden Letters,* 1969

981. The impulse to rewrite, to alter and amend in the colder light of hindsight and maturity, is all but irresistible. Such up-dating and "improvement" would, however, not only be transparently dishonest; it could, I suspect, prove self-defeating.
— GEORGE STEINER, "Introduction to a Reader," June 1983

982. You will observe that my once powerful genius is in a state of pitiable decline. It is true London is rapidly hustling one into the abhorred tomb; I do write such damned rubbish in it.
— ROBERT LOUIS STEVENSON,
letter to Charles Baxter, 1878

983. Since I have been here, I have been toiling like a galley slave
. . . write, rewrite, and re-rewrite.
— ROBERT LOUIS STEVENSON, letter to
Charles Baxter, March 8, 1889

984. I see myself as a typical person who just happens to sit in this room and pound out books because he's basically unemployable.
— TODD STRASSER, in *Behind the Covers* by James Roginski, 1985

985. Even when I write bad books I gain confidence.
— TODD STRASSER, in *Behind the Covers* by James Roginski, 1985

986. I could no longer concentrate during those afternoon hours,

which for years had been my working time, and the act of writing itself, becoming more and more difficult and exhausting, stalled, then finally ceased.
—WILLIAM STYRON, *Darkness Visible: A Memoir of Madness*, 1990

987. We know that sometimes a student learns more from rewriting one piece nine times than from writing nine new things and doing, as he knows, incompetently, similar things over and over.
—ALAN SWALLOW, "Professional Letters and the Teaching of English" in *College Composition and Communication*, May 1960

988. I quarrel at your author, as I do with all writers and many of your preachers, for their careless incorrect and improper style, which they contract by reading the scribblers from England, where an abominable taste is every day prevailing.
—JONATHAN SWIFT, letter to the Rev. Henry Clarke, December 12, 1734

989. Remains a difficulty still,
To purchase Fame by writing ill.
—JONATHAN SWIFT, *On Poetry*, 367–368, 1733

990. An adequate definition of a true critic; that, he is a discoverer and collector of writer's faults.
—JONATHAN SWIFT, *A Tale of a Tub*, 1750

991. My prosebook's going well, but I dislike it. It's the only really dashed-off piece of work I remember doing. It's indecent and trivial, sometimes funny, sometimes mawkish, and always badly written which I do not mind so much.
—DYLAN THOMAS, letter to Vernon Watkins, May 22, 1941

992. Don't be too harsh to these poems until they're typed. I always think typescript lends some sort of certainty: at least, if the things are bad then, they appear to be bad with conviction.
—DYLAN THOMAS, letter to Vernon Watkins, March 1938

993. He [Shakespeare] does, at least, take the reader by the scruff of the neck and push him forward to a definite end, but where on earth your heros are headed for I don't know.
—TOLSTOY, on Chekhov as related by André Maurois in *The Art of Writing*, 1960

994. I do not think that the writing of a novel is the most difficult task which a man may be called upon to do.
— ANTHONY TROLLOPE, *Autobiography*, 1883

995. American students have created a cult around the film [*Casablanca*], principally its dialogue, which they know by heart.
— FRANÇOIS TRUFFAUT, letter to Simon Benzahein, March 10, 1974

996. These stories are so large; they're so wholehearted. Plainly, he never set out to write a mere short story. It was all or nothing.
— ANNE TYLER, on Wallace Stegner,
New York Times Book Review, March 18, 1990

997. Computers bring writing within the scope of what very young children can do. It is far easier to press keys on a keyboard than to control a pencil. Electronic keyboards can be made sensitive to the lightest touch; more important, they permit instant erasure. The computer is a forgiving writing instrument, much easier to use than even an electric typewriter. . . .
Many people are excited by the possibility that writing may be brought within the range of capabilities of very young children. But others seem to feel that setting a four-year-old to writing does violence to a natural process of unfolding. For them, what is most disturbing about [the girl] is not her relationship to the machine, but her relationship to writing, to the abstract, to the symbolic.
— SHERRY TURKLE, *The Second Self*, 1984

998. I want to write about love — about being a human being — about loneliness — about being a woman. I want to write about an encounter on an island. A man who changed my life. I want to write about a change that was accidental and a change that was deliberate. I want to write about moments I regard as gifts, good moments and bad moments. I don't believe that the knowledge or experience that is part of me is any greater than what others have. . . . It is not Liv Ullmann people meet in magazines and newspapers that I shall be writing about. . . . I feel that I am afraid of revealing myself. Afraid that what I write will leave me vulnerable and no longer able to defend myself.
— LIV ULLMANN, *Changing*, 1976

999. Everyday I try to write. It is most difficult at home, where there are telephone calls, Linn, nursemaids, neighbors. . . . Try telling a child that Mamma is working, when the child can see with its own eyes that she is just sitting there writing. . . .

These are my thoughts as I try to write about how good it is to have a life that gives so much freedom, so many choices: I can be free by my own will, be my own creator and guide. My growth and my development depend on what I choose or discard in life. In me are the seeds of my future life.
— LIV ULLMAN, *Changing*, 1976

1000. I discovered as I began to write how delicious the present tense is. . . . Action takes on a wholly different, flickering quality; thought and feeling and event are brought much closer together. And so the present tense proved to be a happy one and I wrote on and on.
— JOHN UPDIKE, *New York Times Book Review*, October 5, 1990

1001. People are programmed, just like computers with this tape feeding out. When I was teaching student writers, I suddenly realized in most cases what I was doing was reaching into the mouth, taking hold of the piece of tape, pulling gently to see if I could read what was printed on it.
— KURT VONNEGUT, JR., interview in *The New Fiction*, 1974

1002. I never learned anything about writing in school and was never greatly interested in my composition courses because I was generally asked to write on an assigned subject, which I could never do. I always had to find my subject for myself.
— EDWARD WAGENKNECHT, interview, *Boston University Alumni Today*, November/December 1990

1003. What the finger writes the soul can read.
— ALICE WALKER, "What the Finger Writes," in *Revolutionary Petunias and Other Poems*, 1973

1004. Writing about people helps us to understand them, and understanding them helps us to accept them as part of ourselves.
— ALICE WALKER, *Living by the Word*, 1984

1005. Writing a song is like writing a letter in care of general delivery. Maybe somebody will call there to pick it up. Maybe not. Sometimes it goes to the dead letter office.
— JIMMY WALKER, attributed by Gene Fowler in *Beau James*, 1949

1006. I was driven into writing because I found it was the only way a lazy and ill-educated man could make a decent living.
— EVELYN WAUGH, *Nash's Pall Mall Magazine*, March 1937

1007. Delay is natural to a writer. He is like a surfer—he bides his time, waits for the perfect wave on which to ride in. Delay is instinctive with him. He waits for the surge (of emotion? of strength? of courage?) that will carry him along. I have no warm-up exercises, other than to take an occasional drink. I am apt to let something simmer for a while in my mind before trying to put it into words . . . I revise a great deal. I know when something is right because bells begin ringing and lights flash. I'm not at all sure what the "necessary equipment" is for a writer—it seems to vary greatly with the individual. Some writers are equipped with extrasensory perception. Some have a good ear, like O'Hara. Some are equipped with humor—although not really as many as think they are. Some are equipped with a massive intellect like Wilson. Some are prodigious. I do think the ability to evaluate one's own stuff with reasonable accuracy is a helpful piece of equipment.

—E. B. WHITE, "Writers at Work,"
Paris Review Interviews, 8th Series, 1988

1008. Writing as a factor in human experience is comparable to the steam-engine. It is important, modern, and artificial.

—ALFRED NORTH WHITEHEAD, *Modes of Thought*, 1938

1009. The greatest [writers] give the impression that their style was nursed by the closest attention to colloquial speech.

—THORNTON WILDER, "Becoming a Writer"
from *Writers at Work*, 1959

1010. "And what are you going to write about, dear?"

"My dear aunt, one doesn't write about anything, one just writes."

Orwell, recalling the joke from Punch, thought it was a "perfectly justified criticism of current literary cant."

—RAYMOND WILLIAMS, *Writing in Society*, 1983

1011. The narrative manner of Defoe has a naturalness about it, beyond that of any other novel or romance writer. His fictions have all the air of true stories. It is impossible to believe, while you are reading them, that a real person is not narrating to you.

—LAMB'S CRITICISM from Walter Wilson's
Memoirs of Life and Times of Daniel Defoe, 1830, 1970

1012. It is the habit of modern criticism to condemn the author of the book criticized for not being the author of someone else's book.

—P. G. WODEHOUSE, *Mulliner Nights*, 1933

1013. If one has written it once, one has said it as well as one can — for ever.
—P. G. WODEHOUSE, *Mulliner Nights*, 1933

1014. In the novel she had elaborated this quarrel, which in fact had lasted twenty-three minutes into a ten years' estrangement—thus justifying the title and preventing the story finishing in the first five thousand words.
—P. G. WODEHOUSE, *Mulliner Nights*, 1933

1015. Ye who do songs of love endite
Knoweth not well of that ye write.
—JOHN WOLCOTT, "To Authors," *The Works of Peter Pindar*, 1812

1016. I'm writing a long play now that has gripped my heart and soul. I worked for months for an idea but none would come.
—THOMAS WOLFE, letter to his mother, March 1921

1017. Stanley folds sentences inside sentences and pushes things further than they have any business being pushed.
—GEOFFREY WOLFF, on Stanley Elkin,
New York Times, March 3, 1991

1018. It is doubtful whether in the course of the centuries, though we have learnt much about making machines, we have learnt anything about making literature. We do not come to write better; all that we can be said to do is keep moving, now a little in this direction, now in that, but with a circular tendency.
—VIRGINIA WOOLF, "Modern Fiction," *The Common Reader*, 1925

1019. If a writer were a free man and not a slave, if he could write what he chose, not what he must, if he could base his work upon his own feeling and not upon convention, there would be no plot, no comedy, no tragedy, no love interest or catastrophe.
—VIRGINIA WOOLF, "Modern Fiction," *The Common Reader*, 1925

1020. I wanted to try to build a bridge of words between me and that world outside, that world which was so distant and elusive that it seemed unreal.
—RICHARD WRIGHT, *American Hunger*, 1977

1021. He was interested in everything, and, everywhere he went, book ideas popped out of him.
—*Buz Wyeth*, on Cass Canfield, Jr.,
Publishers Weekly, January 19, 1990

1022. Lies written in ink can never disguise facts written in blood.
— LU XUN, quoted in *The New York Times Book Review*, August 19, 1990

1023. As you go on writing and thinking your ideas will arrange themselves. They will arrange themselves as sand strewn upon stretched parchment does — as I have read somewhere — in response to a musical note.
— W. B. YEATS, letter to Dorothy Wellesley, July 26, 1935

1024. Writing is a physical activity. The pen gives voice to the hand. Each written word is connected to the writer both through the immediate physical relationship of fingers and pen. In the art of writing there is a part of the self that is invested in and so identified with the thing written. It comes to be experienced as an extension of the self rather than an "otherness." This identification occurs so subtly, that it is rarely noticed until it has been taken away. Electronic text confronts [us] with a stark sense of otherness. Text is impersonal; letters and numbers seem to appear without having been derived from an embodied process of authorship. They stand autonomously over and against [the person] who engages with them.
— SHOSHANA ZUBOFF, *In the Age of the Smart Machine*, 1988

1025. I like writing to you in the same way as you do to me and I don't like letting a machine intervene in our warm personal contact with each other.
— ARNOLD ZWEIG, letter to Sigmund Freud, September 8, 1930

1026. The art of the pen is to rouse the inward vision. . . . That is why the poets, who spring imagination with a word or a phrase, paint lasting pictures.
— GEORGE MEREDITH, *Diana of the Crossways*, 1885

1027. All writing comes by the grace of God.
— EMERSON, essay, "Experience," 1847

1028. No man can write anything who does not think that what he writes is, for the time, the history of the world.
— EMERSON, essay, "Nature," 1847

1029. Dear authors! suit your topics to your strength
And ponder well your subject and its length
Nor lift your load, before you're quite aware
What weight your shoulders will, or will not, bear.
— LORD BYRON, *Hints from Horace*, line 59, 1821

1030. Choose a subject, ye who write,
Suited to your strength.
—HORACE, *The Art of Poetry*, line 38

1031. Look, then, into thine heart and write.
—LONGFELLOW, *Voices of the Night:* Prelude, st. 19

1032. Do not seek to render word for word
Like a slavish translator.
—HORACE, *The Art of Poetry*, line 133

1033. Modern writers are the moons of literature; they shine with reflected light, with light borrowed from the ancients.
—SAMUEL JOHNSON, *Boswell's Life of Johnson*,
Wednesday, April 29, 1778

1034. Let us consider the false appearance
That are imposed on us by words.
—FRANCIS BACON, *Advancement of Learning*, Book II, XIV, 11

1035. Among all kinds of writing, there is none in which authors are more apt to miscarry than in works of humor, as there is none in which they are more ambitious to excel.
—JOSEPH ADDISON, *The Spectator*, April 10, 1711

1036. Between the reputation of the author living and the reputation of the same author dead there is ever a wide discrepancy.
—THOMAS BAILEY ALDRICH, *Ponkapog Papers*, 1903

1037. For the creation of a master-work of literature two powers must concur, the power of the man and the power of the moment and the man is not enough without the moment.
—MATTHEW ARNOLD, *The Function of Criticism*, 1864

1038. No poet or novelist wishes he were the only one who ever lived, but most of them wish they were the only one alive, and quite a number believe their wish has been granted.
—W. H. AUDEN, "Writing," *The Dyer's Hand*, 1962

1039. Many a fervid man
Writes books as cold and flat
as graveyard stones...
—ELIZABETH BARRETT BROWNING, "Aurora Leigh," 1856

1040. Of writing many books there is no end;
And I, who have written much in
prose and verse
For others uses, will write now for mine
Will write my story for my better self.
—ELIZABETH BARRETT BROWNING, "Aurora Leigh," 1856

1041. There's more than passion goes to make a man
Or book, which is a man, too.
—ELIZABETH BARRETT BROWNING, "Aurora Leigh," 1856

1042. To be a well-favored man is the gift of fortune; but to write
and read comes by nature.
—SHAKESPEARE, *Much Ado About Nothing*, III, ii

1043. Write down the advice of him who loves you, though you
like it not at present.
— 17TH CENTURY PROVERB, *Everyman's Dictionary
of Quotations and Proverbs*, 1951

1044. Think much, speak little, and write less.
—ITALIAN PROVERB, *Everyman's Dictionary
of Quotations and Proverbs*, 1951

1045. Let there be gall enough in thy ink, though thou write with
a goose pen.
—SHAKESPEARE, *Twelfth Night*, III, ii

1046. Words, words, whose separate meanings
must go wide
Unless the visionary
Compose them, so his eyes are satisfied.
—BABETTE DEUTSCH, "The Poem," in *The Collected Poems*, 1969

1047. Revolutions do not start in bomb factories. They start in
inkpots.
—FRANCIS HACKETT, *On Judging Books*, 1947

1048. There was a time when books
were so valuable it was
dangerous to have them.
—FREDERIC ROWLAND MARVIN,
The Companionship of Books, 1905

1049. I've been overlooking the German translation of my books beginning with "Chopin." Bored to death! I hate rereading my rubbish.
— JAMES GIBBONS HUNEHER, letter to Emma Eames,
June 21, 1913

1050. I find a conversational tone in writing—as in telephoning—carries further than shouting.
— JAMES GIBBONS HUNEHER, letter to Emma Eames,
June 21, 1913

1051. The old fashioned ideas of "inspiration," spontaneity, easy improvisation, the sudden bolt from heaven, are delusions still hugged by the world.
— JAMES GIBBONS HUNEHER, *The Baudelaire Legend*, 1929

1052. The wisdom of the wise, and the experience of ages, may be preserved by quotation.
— ISAAC DISRAELI, Quotation, *Curiosities of Literature*, 1860

1053. Aristotle, it will be remembered, does not employ the word "fancy" or "imagination" at all in the *Poetics*.
— IRVING BABBITT, "Dr. Johnson and Imagination"
in *On Being Creative*, 1932

1054. Maybe later if my books become popular in France I will again try to write what I want. But now I am just trying to keep alive.
— CHESTER HIMES, *My Life of Absurdity*, 1976

1055. The mountain vocabulary at its best, in exact, specific words, and illuminating images and phrases, is far richer and more flexible than that of the average university graduate.
— PERCY MACKAYE, Preface to *This Fine-Pretty World*, 1924

1056. If I were absolutely honest in making out a list of the books which have helped me I think I should head the list with Noah Webster's famous Unabridged Dictionary.
— PHILIP S. MARDEN, *Detours*, 1926

1057. It is essentially a book of today. It is alive and warm. It is brutal with life. It is written of sweat, and blood and groans and tears.
— JACK LONDON, on Upton Sinclair's *The Jungle*, 1905

1058. It is the poet alone can touch with words.
— JOHN LOGAN, "To a Young Poet Who Fled"
from *Spring of the Thief*, 1963

1059. It taught me to shape a story and to hold in mind what I had thought up; so it fostered facility. On the other hand, it taught me to use exaggerated phrases and clichés, and this is something I have fought against, not always successfully. This writing is an unnatural business; it makes your head hot and your feet cold, and it stops the digestion of your food.

— UPTON SINCLAIR, quoting John Burroughs
in *Autobiography*, 1962

1060. The English language is no whore.

— GENEVIEVE TAGGARD, "To Mr. Maudner,"
Professional Poet, 1927

1061. Gustave Flaubert created the modern novel.
Gustave Flaubert created the modern short story.
He created both because he created modern fiction.

— ALLEN TATE, *Techniques of Fiction*, 1944

1062. In order to write anything serious I should have to write a volume, and for that I have not time.

— THEODORE ROOSEVELT, letter to Upton Sinclair, July 7, 1915

1063. How can you contrive to write so even?

— JANE AUSTEN, *Pride and Prejudice*, 1813

1064. You are really proud of your defects in writing, because you consider them as proceeding from a rapidity of thought.

— JANE AUSTEN, *Pride and Prejudice*, 1813

1065. I think I may boast myself to be, with all possible vanity, the most unlearned and uninformed female who ever dared to be an authoress.

— JANE AUSTEN, letter to James Clarke, December 11, 1815

1066. I wish you wouldn't insist on writing separately.

— OWEN ROBERTS, entry in the diary of
Felix Frankfurter, February 6, 1943

1067. Many American writers are vicarious detectives; Tom Craig is a detective who can write.

— WILLIAM BRADFORD AUIE, Acknowledgements in
The Execution of Private Slovik, January 21, 1954

1068. While other words may mean different things, a proper name means one person or thing and no other.
— OLIVER WENDELL HOLMES, *Theory of Legal Interpretation*, 1899

1069. The idealists give away their case when they write books.
— OLIVER WENDELL HOLMES, *Ideals and Doubts*, 1915

1070. We do not read novels for improvement or instruction.
— OLIVER WENDELL HOLMES, remarks at the Tavern Club, March 4, 1900

1071. I never dare to write as funny as I can.
— OLIVER WENDELL HOLMES, SR., *The Height of the Ridiculous*, circa 1830

1072. Take, then, this treasure to thy trust,
To win some idle reader's smile,
Then fade and moulder in the dust,
Or swell some bonfire's pile.
— OLIVER WENDELL HOLMES, SR., "To a Blank Piece of Paper," 1830

1073. There are books that make one feel as if he were in his dressing gown and slippers.
— OLIVER WENDELL HOLMES, "Pillow Smoothing Authors," *Atlantic Monthly*, April, 1883

1074. I always pity a fine old volume which has fallen into poor company, and sometimes buy it even if I do not want it, that it may find itself once more among its peers.
— OLIVER WENDELL HOLMES, "Pillow Smoothing Authors," *Atlantic Monthly*, April, 1883

1075. To write a verse or two is all the praise
That I can raise.
— GEORGE HERBERT, *The Church from the Temple*, 1633

1076. Where's the fault? Not in our books
No sure, 't is in yourself
I'll tell you why, sir
Books give not wisdom where was none before
But where some is, there reading makes it more.
— SIR JOHN HARRINGTON, *Epigrams*, Book I, No. 3, circa 1615

1077. The readers, and the hearers like my books
But yet some Writers cannot them digest
But what care I? For when I make a feast
I would my guests should praise it, not the cooks.
—SIR JOHN HARRINGTON, *Epigrams*, Book I, No. 6, circa 1615

1078. This is some of our new florid language, and the graces and delicacies of style, which, if it were put into Latin, I would fain know which is the principal verb.
—DANIEL DEFOE, "Of Academics" from
An Essay Upon Projects, 1697

1079. If you can but contrive to be tired of reading as soon as I am tired of writing, we shall find that short ones answer just as well.
—WILLIAM COWPER, letter to Joseph Hill, July 3, 1765

1080. And face them, though it were in spite
Of nature and their stars, to write.
—SAMUEL BUTLER, *Hudibras*, Part I, Canto I, lines 641–642, 1662

1081. Poetry is much an easier and more agreeable species of composition than prose, and could a man live by it, it were no unpleasant employment to be a poet.
—OLIVER GOLDSMITH, letter to Henry Goldsmith,
January 13, 1759

1082. The poet by nature comes forth a poet from his mother's womb and, following the bent that heaven has bestowed on him, without the aid of study or art, he produces things that show how truly he spoke who said, "Est Deus in nobis."
—MIGUEL DE CERVANTES, *Don Quixote*, Part II, Chpt. XVI, 1605

1083. One of the things that ought to give most pleasure to a virtuous and eminent man is to find himself in his lifetime in print and in type.
—MIGUEL DE CERVANTES, *Don Quixote*, Part II, Chpt. III, 1605

1084. The poet may describe or sing things, not as they are, but as they ought to have been, while the historian has to write them down, not as they ought to have been, but as they were.
—MIGUEL DE CERVANTES, *Don Quixote*, Part II, Chpt. III, 1605

1085. There are some who write and toss out books as if they were fritters.
—MIGUEL DE CERVANTES, *Don Quixote*, Part II, Chpt. III, 1605

1086. Go forth my book into the open day.
— ROBERT BURTON, *The Anatomy of Melancholy*, 1621

1087. Our writings are as so many dishes, our readers guests, our books like beauty, that which one admires another rejects.
— ROBERT BURTON, *The Anatomy of Melancholy*, 1621

1088. What epigrams are in poetry, the same are ayres in music, then in their chief perfection when they are short and well seasoned.
— THOMAS CAMPION, *A Book of Ayres*, 1601

1089. Enough words; there are too many to burden this little book.
— THOMAS CAMPION, *The Second Book
of Epigrams*, No. 228, 1619

1090. I heartily wish this play were as perfect as I intended it.
— WILLIAM CONGREVE, letter to Charles Montagu,
December 7, 1693

1091. His memory, miraculously great
Could plots exceeding man's belief repeat;
Which therefore cannot be accounted lies,
For human wit could never such devise.
— JOHN DRYDEN, *Absalom and Achitophel*, lines 650–653

1092. All this time I had been writing stories, plays, essays. But it was years before anything came of it.
— JEROME K. JEROME, *My Life and Times*, 1926

1093. I wonder if the smart journalists who make fun in the comic papers of the rejected contributor have ever been themselves through that torture-chamber.
— JEROME K. JEROME, *My Life and Times*, 1926

1094. Not the writing merely, but what a man writes, make him an object of interest to me.
— CHARLES KINGSLEY, letter to
the Rev. J. Montagu, November 30, 1865

1095. I don't agree with you about not polishing too much. If you are a verse maker, you will, of course, rub off the edges and the silvering; but if you are a poet and have an idea and one keynote running through the whole, which you can't for the life define to yourself but

which is there out of the abysses, defining you, then every polishing is a bringing the thing nearer to that idea.
— CHARLES KINGSLEY, letter to Mr. Ludlow, June 1852

1096. I sabotage the sentence! With me is the naked word, I spike the verb — all parts of speech are pushed over on their backs.
— WYNDHAM LEWIS, "One Way Song"
from *The Lion and the Fox*, 1927

1097. A great many clever critics who are more concerned with displaying their intellectual numbness than with maintaining any critical standards try to gain a reputation for wit by poking fun at unfamiliar excellence.
— JOHN PRESS, *The Chequer'd Shade*, 1958

1098. I take it in fact to be always necessary, whenever ideas are expressed in proper and appropriate language, that no word should be more dignified than the nature of the ideas.
— DIONYSIUS OF HALICARNASSUS, *De Compositione Verborum*, Chapter III

1099. Shakespeare, writing his *King Lear*, was evidently in some sort of trance.
— WYNDHAM LEWIS, *Time and Western Man*, 1927

1100. Then there are other cases where the writer is giving a narrative about a person, and by a sudden transition himself passes into that person.
— LONGINUS, *Concerning Sublimity*, XXVII

1101. For beautiful words are, in a real and special sense, the light of thought.
— LONGINUS, *Concerning Sublimity*, XXX

1102. There is enough in the novel to have made success fairly sure, if some judicious friend has revised the manuscript.
— WILLIAM SHARP, *The Life and Letters of Joseph Severn*, 1892

1103. The idea of writing down my memories rather smiles upon me. It is pleasant to wander down the lanes of yesterday into the land of long ago and to bring back tales.
— W. GRAHAM ROBERTSON, *Life Was Worth Living*, 1931

1104. A woman and a book are not the same thing, even though you can sometimes take both of them to bed.
— G. LEGMAN, *The Horn Book*, 1964

1105. Reasoning is but words.
— DOROTHY L. SAYERS, *The Emperor Constantine: A Chronicle*, 1951

1106. I find that having an editor in the family has many compensations, along with a few drawbacks.
— CATHERINE MARSHALL, *Beyond Our Selves*, 1961

1107. A double noose thou on thy neck dost pull
For writing treason, and for writing dull.
— JOHN DRYDEN, *Absalom and Achitophel*, II, lines 496–497, 1682

1108. Drink, swear and roar, forbear no lewd delight
Fit for thy bulk, do any thing but write.
— JOHN DRYDEN, *Absalom and Achitophel*, II, lines 478–479, 1682

1109. And such he needs must be of thy inditing,
This comes of drinking asses' milk and writing.
— JOHN DRYDEN, *Absalom and Achitophel*, II, lines 394–395, 1682

1110. Pardon this paper and vile writing; I am forced to scribble on as fast as possible, not to lose so good an opportunity.
— FANNY BURNEY, letter to Queen Charlotte, April 21, 1802

1111. The more the book is drawn into notice, the more exposed it becomes to criticism and remark.
— FANNY BURNEY, diary, June 18, 1778

1112. A clever man could adopt these ready-made plots and characters, amend the style, eliminate the absurdities, supply the missing links — and the result would be a splendid original novel.
— ALEXANDER PUSHKIN, *A Novel in Letters*, 1829

1113. Some readers will perhaps wish to know my opinion of Pichorin's character. . . . My answer is the title of this book.
— VASCO PRATOLINI, quoting Mikhail Lermontov's
A Hero of Our Time in *A Hero of Our Time*, 1951

1114. Russian fiction is like German music — the best in the world.
— WILLIAM LYON PHELPS, *Essays on Russian Novelists*, 1911

1115. I have gone through much in myself; and now there are things I am going to see and go through. There will be much to be written.
— FYODOR DOSTOEVSKY, attributed to him
by A. P. Milivkov in *Reminiscences*, 1891

1116. The same thing has been printed and read a thousand times before.
— FYODOR DOSTOEVSKY, *Crime and Punishment*,
Part III, Chapter 5, 1866

1117. The moment I took up the pen, I began to be afraid.
— FYODOR DOSTOEVSKY, *The Diary of a Writer*, February 1876

1118. Even this must have a preface — that is, a literary preface.
— FYODOR DOSTOEVSKY, "The Grand Inquisitor,"
The Brothers Karamazov, 1879

1119. The itch for writing and making a name holds you fast as with a noose, and becomes inveterate in your distempered brain.
— JUVENAL, *Satires*, VII, 52

1120. On a winter's night when wind and rain rage with a sullen roar,
With a pipe, a book, a blazing fire,
What does a man want more?
— GEORGE PHILLIPS AND W. R. SIMMONS,
A Dickens's Monologue, 1910

1121. All other trades demand, verse-makers beg.
— EDWARD YOUNG, *Love of Fame*, Satire IV, verse 191, 1728

1122. "How do I know," the sometimes despairing writer asks, "which the right word is?" The reply must be: only you can know. The right word is, simply, the wanted one; the wanted word is the one most nearly true.
— ELIZABETH BOWEN, *Afterthoughts: Pieces on Writing*, 1962

1123. Verbs first appear with the flowers who utter imperative odors.
— W. H. AUDEN, "Natural Linguistics" in *Epistle to a Godson*, 1969

1124. When reading a scholarly critic, one profits more from his quotations than from his comments.
— W. H. AUDEN, "Reading," *The Dyer's Hand*, 1962

1125. More than ever now
I sometimes think no poetry is read.
— RUPERT BROOKE, *A Letter to a Live Poet*, 1915

1126. In your diary, as in mine, there are days marked with sadness, not this year only, but for all.
— WILLIAM MAKEPEACE THACKERY, on Lett's diary
in *Roundabout Papers*, 1860

1127. There is another evil which I complain of, that this system of newspaper writing spoils one for every other kind of writing.
— WILLIAM MAKEPEACE THACKERY, letter to
Mrs. Carmichael-Smyth, September 6, 1833

1128. There are two ways of misunderstanding a poem. One is to misunderstand it and the other to praise it for qualities that it does not possess.
— OSCAR WILDE, *The Moods of a Man of Letters*, 1916

1129. Some passages of mine . . . I rewrote a dozen times. . . . You cannot write well and forcibly without at times writing flatly, and the real quality of a writer is, like divinity, inalienable.
— H. G. WELLS, *Experiment in Autobiography*, 1934

1130. A real writer is always shifting and changing and searching.
— JAMES BALDWIN, *Nobody Knows My Name*, 1961

1131. The writer's greed is appalling. He wants, or seems to want, everything and practically everybody; in another sense, and at the same time, he needs no one at all.
— JAMES BALDWIN, *Nobody Knows My Name*, 1961

1132. The avowed aim of the American protest novel is to bring greater freedom to the oppressed.
— JAMES BALDWIN, *Notes of a Native Son*, 1955

1133. When we write from personal experience, we can write more fluently and freely.
— DIETRICH BONHOEFFER, letter to his parents, June 4, 1943

1134. He cannot write, who knows not to give o'er,
To mend one fault, he makes a hundred more.
— BOILEAU, *The Art of Poetry*, 1674

1135. In writing, vary your discourse and phrase
A frozen style that neither ebbs or flows,
Instead of pleasing, makes us gape and doze.
— BOILEAU, *The Art of Poetry*, 1674

1136. Writing means revealing oneself to excess.
— FRANZ KAFKA, letter to Felice, January 14, 1913

1137. One can never be alone enough when one writes.
— FRANZ KAFKA, letter to Felice, January 14, 1913

1138. Who often reads, will sometimes wish to write.
— GEORGE CRABBE, *Tales: Edward Shore*, line 109, 1812

1139. It is a classic instance of the maxim that literary works are made out of other literary works.
— DONALD R. HOWARD, about Coleridge's
"Kubla Khan" in *Writers and Pilgrims*, 1980

1140. Quotations are of two sorts, not including misquotations, which are far commoner, and of which there are, therefore, more varieties. They may be frankly acknowledged . . . they may be adroitly hidden.
— HERBERT PAUL, *Men and Letters*, 1901

1141. A banished writer, one of the best, scanning the list of the burned, was shocked to find that his books had been passed over.
— BERTOLT BRECHT, *The Burning of the Books*, 1936

1142. How long do works endure? As long
As they are not completed,
Since as long as they demand effort
They do not decay.
— BERTOLT BRECHT, "About the Way
to Construct Enduring Works," 1929

1143. It seemed to me, as with almost all my writings when I reread them after a long time, a bit too long, a bit too talkative, perhaps the same thing is said too often in somewhat different words.
— HERMANN HESSE, *Events in the Engadine*, 1953

1144. Never forget that writing is as close as we get to keeping a hold on the thousand and one things.
— SALMAN RUSHDIE, Introduction to Gunter Grass'
On Writing and Politics, 1985

1145. The manuscripts of the first, second, and finally third drafts fed the furnace that was located in my workroom.

—GUNTER GRASS, *The Tin Drum in Retrospect or The Author as Dubious Witness*, 1974

1146. The story which this book essays to tell is not of the teller's choosing. It simply came, with supreme indifference to other plans, and autocratically demanded right of way.

—JOHN LIVINGSTON LOWES, Preface to *The Road to Xanadu*, January 10, 1927

1147. One ought not to write a commentary on one's own work.

—ARTHUR CHRISTOPHER BENSON, *Escape and Other Essays*, 1915

1148. Even when the characters are making what are evidently to them perfectly natural and straightforward remarks, I do not feel sure what they mean; and I suffer paroxysms of rage as I read, because I feel that I cannot get at what is there without a mental agility which seems to me unnecessarily fatiguing. A novel ought to be like a walk.

—ARTHUR CHRISTOPHER BENSON, *The Upton Letters*, August 27, 1904

1149. It is my misfortune to have been under the necessity too often of writing rapidly, and without opportunities for after-revision.

—THOMAS DE QUINCEY, *Letter to a Young Man*, IV, 1823

1150. The poet who seeks to be representative must, like Homer, know how to tell lies skilfully [sic]. He must, in short, be a master of illusion.

—IRVING BABBITT, *On Being Creative*, 1932

1151. It has become difficult to imagine literature without love.

—JOHN BAGLEY, *The Characters of Love*, 1960

1152. When once the itch of literature comes over a man, nothing can cure it but the scratching of a pen. But if you have not a pen, I suppose you must scratch any way you can.

—SAMUEL LOVER, *Handy Andy*, Chapter 36, 1842

1153. Several different writers have been made responsible for that book, and I happen to be personally acquainted with four historians who have discovered its true author; unfortunately, no two of them have discovered the same.

—ETIENNE GILSON, *Reason and Revelation in the Middle Ages*, 1938

1154. If you wish him to read, you must make reading pleasant. You must give him short views, and clear sentences. It will not answer to explain what all the things which you describe are not. You must begin by saying what they are.
— WALTER BEGEHOT, *The First Edinburgh Reviews*, 1855

1155. Reviews are, as Coleridge declared, a species of maggots, inferior to bookworms, living on the delicious brains of real genius.
— WALTER BEGEHOT, *The First Edinburgh Reviews*, 1855

1156. The first play I wrote never left the drawer. The second, a three-character comedy, made it to Off-Broadway — for just one night.
— JERRY STERNER, "Playwright or Businessman,"
New York Times Magazine, June 9, 1991

1157. Don't worry about errors when you're writing. The biographers will explain all errors.
— HENRY MILLER, *Black Spring*, 1963

1158. What the Popes mumbled in their beards is one thing — what they commanded to be painted on their walls is another. Words are dead.
— HENRY MILLER, *Black Spring*, 1963

1159. Sometimes titles are written to books and sometimes books are written to titles.
— FRANCES PARKINSON KEYES, author's note to
The River Road, September 1945

1160. There is no past or future in the grammar of God.
— JOHN GARDNER, "The Warden" in *The King's Indian*, 1972

1161. Some poets get to the heart of the matter. Most just fool around with the language.
— JOHN GARDNER, "The Warden" in *The King's Indian*, 1972

1162. It was virtually impossible to get hold of a book and that, if you did, you could read it only on the sly.
— FYODOR DOSTOEVSKY, letter to M. M. Dostoevsky,
February 22, 1854

1163. I have been too often forced to write very, very poor pieces because I have had to hurry to meet deadlines.
— FYODOR DOSTOEVSKY, letter to M. N. Katkov,
September 1865

1164. In 20 years of writing, producing and directing comedy, I never once read a book about it. Prior to that, the longest time I ever went without reading a book was perhaps the four years I spent in college.
— DAVID ZUCKER, *New York Times*, June 23, 1991

1165. Then we'd revise, make the words walk slowly on the slippery train.
— JUDITH SMALL, "Body of Work," *The New Yorker*, July 8, 1991

1166. It's o.k. to split infinitives under certain circumstances. After all, hard-core hostility to the practice was not expressed in English usage manuals until late in the 19th century.
— CHRISTOPHER LEHMAN-HAUPT, *New York Times*, July 4, 1991

1167. Writing is what I do. I have to do it.
— JAMES MICHENER, *The Novel*, 1991

1168. Writing a novel, like making chicken soup or making love, is an idiosyncratic occupation; probably no two people do it the same way.
— SUSAN ISAACS, *New York Times Book Review*, March 31, 1991

1169. My real name is Lillian. It was part of becoming a writer, not becoming the person I was supposed to be.
— GISH JEN, on changing her name,
New York Times Book Review, March 31, 1991

1170. The poetic . . . depends on a half-voluntary, half-involuntary, integration of the conscious will with other factors in the psyche, factors connected with fantasy, dreaming let's pretend.
— NORTHROP FRYE, *Words with Power*, 1991

1171. Why not tell one's story? There are so few stories here, or perhaps a fear of telling. I myself forget much.
— SHIRLEY HAZZARD, "In These Islands,"
The New Yorker, June 18, 1990

1172. How do you write fiction (or poetry, for that matter) about painters and dancers and writers and musicians? . . . Writers pretend to be inarticulate, painters speak in symbols or hyperbole, musicians gossip and tell jokes, dancers talk about their bodies and about food. There is an added difficulty in writing fiction about jazz: the music is ephemeral.
— WHITNEY BALLIETT, "Imaging Music," *The New Yorker*, June 18, 1990

1173. All works of the past continually require reconsideration, whether or not gender is the issue. (Any history of taste recalls that for centuries "Gothic" was a term of critical contempt.) Rereading neglected women writers may give us fresh insights into the concerns of half our species and into the development of literary audiences.
— NAOMI BLIVEN, "Old Pros," *The New Yorker*, March 25, 1991

1174. Or a long sentence moving at a certain pace down the page aiming for the bottom — if not the bottom of this page then of some other page — where it can rest, or stop for a moment to think about the questions raised by its own (temporary) existence, which ends when the page is turned.
— DONALD BARTHELME, "Sentence," *City Life*, 1968

1175. I knew I should write but I had let it go so long that it was almost impossible to write now. There was nothing to write about.
— ERNEST HEMINGWAY, *A Farewell to Arms*, 1929

1176. Maybe if it's raining and I'm in the bedroom with the curtains closed but still hearing the rain, then an old book is o.k., especially if it smells stale and has that thick, brittle paper.
— FREDERICH BARTHELME, "Margaret and Bud,"
The New Yorker, June 3, 1991

1177. I am not a professional writer; I am not even a skilled writer; I am just a writer who is on the way to learning his profession.
— THOMAS WOLFE, *The Story of a Novel*, 1936

1178. What never works: the novel which is more at the mercy of social thesis than an impulse of art.
— PAUL HORGAN, "Approaches to Writing," *Notebook Pages*, 1973

1179. I said I had already used every single thing I knew about the Yiddish theater to write one story, and I didn't have time to learn any more, then write about it. There is a long time in me between knowing and telling.
— GRACE PALEY, *Debts*, 1960–1974

1180. I don't know anything about fingerprinting or ballistics or any of that stuff, and if you're any good you can fake most of that. I don't do research.
— ROBERT B. PARKER, interview,
The New York Times Book Review, July 28, 1991

1181. I made every effort to write just like Raymond Chandler.
The degree to which those early books are different is the degree to
which I failed in my attempt.
— ROBERT B. PARKER, interview,
The New York Times Book Review, July 28, 1991

1182. We call some lies "fiction" and maintain, paradoxically, that
they tell the truth. Elaborate, convincing lies (such as novels) over-
whelm us with their scope and coherence, or they seduce us by telling
us what we want to hear, by saying the words we wish were true.
— MATTHEW STADLER, *New York Times
Book Review,* July 28, 1991

1183. To think of a story is much harder work than to write it . . .
to think it over as you lie in bed, or walk about, or sit cozily over your
fire, to turn it all in your thoughts, and make the things fit — that requires
elbow-grease of the mind. The arrangement of the words is as though
you were walking simply along a road. The arrangement of your story
is as though you were carrying a sack of flour while you walked.
— ANTHONY TROLLOPE, in George Levine's *Darwin and
the Novelists: Patterning Science in Victorian Fiction,* 1988

1184. There are simple maxims — not perhaps quite as simple as
those [of others] offered to me — which I think might be commended to
writers of expository prose. First: never use a long word if a short one
will do. Second: if you want to make a statement with a great many
qualifications, put some of the qualifications in separate sentences.
Third: do not let the beginning of your sentence lead the readers to an
expectation which is contradicted by the end.
— BERTRAND RUSSELL, "How I Write"
from *Portraits from Memory,* 1956

1185. Very gradually I have discovered ways of writing with a
minimum of worry and anxiety. When I was young each fresh piece of
serious work used to seem to me . . . to be beyond my powers. . . . I
would make one unsatisfying attempt after another and in the end have
to discard them all. At last I found that such fumbling attempts were a
waste of time. It appeared that after first contemplating a book on some
subject, and after giving serious preliminary attention to it, I need a
period of subconscious incubation which could not be hurried and was,
if anything, impeded by deliberate thinking. Sometimes I would find,
after a time, that I had made a mistake, and that I could not write the
book I had had in mind. But often I was more fortunate. Having, by a

time of very intense concentration, planted the problem in my sub-conscious, it would germinate underground, until, suddenly, the solution emerged with blinding clarity, so that it only remained to write down what had appeared as if in a revelation.
— BERTRAND RUSSELL, "How I Write"
from *Portraits from Memory*, 1956

1186. Within a month, the bulk of the work was finished, and the producers and I reassembled to "polish" the script, a ritual in which anything that might be construed as amusing is painstakingly removed. Steletto was exceptionally skilled at this type of surgery, and from youth his deep distrust of any word of more than two syllables stamped him for future leadership. . . . In due course, the script was hacked and altered beyond recognition, and it was time for the vultures from the advertising agency and the network to descend. Scores of experts flopped in to pontificate on what was wrong with the script . . . and the finished product, sparkling as flavorful as a plate of cold gruel, was ready for the oven.
— S. J. PERELMAN, *Chicken Inspector No. 23*, 1966

1187. Such writing damages the proletarian image, clogs the message with fancy creative-writing-course prose, and is clearly written under the impression that this is how good writers write; Orwell would have seen in it an illustration of what he took to be an inevitable process, the kidnapping of working-class writers by the bourgeoisie the minute they put pen to paper. The only way to write plainly, as a worker should, would be to write like Orwell. But the plain style is a middle-class accomplishment, got by arduous and educated rhetorical efforts. In Jones's posher bits of prose, and his occasional glamorization of the workers, working-class pastoral takes over from proletarian realism; heroic, loving, loyal, and tragic gestures are recorded and admired as if from the outside; fine writing takes place.
— FRANK KERMODE, *History and Value*, 1988

1188. Writing, at its best, is a lonely life. Organizations for writers palliate the writers' loneliness but I doubt if they improve his writing. He grows in public stature as he sheds his loneliness and often his work deteriorates. For he does his work alone and if he is a good enough writer he must face eternity, or the lack of it, each day.
— ERNEST HEMINGWAY, statement to the Swedish Academy on receiving the Nobel Prize quoted in *Hemingway*, Kenneth S. Lynn

1189. What turned out to be a "career" started, so to speak, of itself. It began as I was sitting at my desk, staring at a page of Chinese

characters (I was doing a degree in Chinese), which danced mean-
inglessly across the frail paper . . . it began when, for no reason I can
fathom, a sentence came into my head. "The Lutchmans lived in a part
of the city where the houses, tall and narrow. . . ." I pushed away the
books and papers in front of me, wrote down the sentence and started
to follow it. At that moment I was propelled by inquisitiveness, not by
literary anticipation. I wanted to see where—how far—that sentence
would take me. It took me a long way. To suggest that I left Oxford with
a vocation would be an exaggeration. What I did take with me was a
possibility of further adventure with that sentence which had presented
itself to me so gratuitously. Another two years would pass before it un-
wound itself to a climax, before I could say I had written a "book."
　　　　　　　　　—SHIVA NAIPAUL, *An Unfinished Journey*, 1987

1190. My rebellion against college took other forms. . . . It came
out in a series of attempts to put down on paper an extensive but far
from orderly criticism of what was the matter with education in general,
and with my own education in particular. I still have the fumbling, painfully pretentious beginnings of more than one book on the subject: but
unlike some of my less ambitious notes of the same date, they know only
faint traces of intellectual independence and even fainter traces of coherent thinking.
　　In both content and style these experiments were smudged repro-
ductions of the modern authors I then admired. . . . I cottoned to [Allen]
Upward . . . because he . . . had launched a wholesale attack on Latin
and Greek as a source of spiritual corruption and made an atavistic
effort to set things right by getting back to the original meanings of old
Anglo-Saxon roots. . . .
　　　　　—LEWIS MUMFORD, *Sketches from Life: The Early Years*, 1982

1191. Not the story [*Streetcar Named Desire*] or characters or the
direction, but the words and their liberation, the joy of the writer in
writing them, the radiant eloquence of its composition, moved me more
than all its pathos. . . . With *Streetcar*, Tennessee . . . helped me as I
turned to Willy Loman. . . . I wanted precisely the same fluidity in the
form, and now it was clear to me that this must be primarily verbal. The
language would of course have to be recognizably his to begin with, but
it seemed possible now to infiltrate it with a kind of superconscious-
ness. . . . I started writing one morning . . . and I wrote all day until
dark, and then I had dinner and went back and wrote until some hour
in the darkness.
　　　　　　　　　　　—ARTHUR MILLER, *Timebends*, 1987

1192. Each young and ardent person writes a diary, in which, when the hours of prayer and penitence arrive, he inscribes his soul. The pages thus written are to him burning and fragrant.
— RALPH WALDO EMERSON, "Nature," 1847

1193. In reality they are more precise than any version of language could be, and they embrace, moreover, a great deal more besides.
— COUNT HERMANN KEYSERLING, *The Travel Diary of a Philosopher*, Vol. II, 37, 1925

1194. I did keep a diary during my last year at school but when I re-read it a year or two later I was so embarrassed by its callowness that I threw it away.
— A. J. AYER, *Part of My Life*, 1977

1195. Everything I have written down in book form was initially jotted down in notebooks or on loose sheets of paper, and the innumerable individual characters were indeed written by my own hand. Is this perhaps a clue? Am I in the final analysis my hand?
— GABRIEL MARCEL, "Searching," *My Dramatic Works as Viewed by a Philosopher*, 1964

1196. I have finished my new novel—"The Third Violet"—and sent it to Appletone and Co., as per request, but I've an idea it won't be accepted. It's pretty rotten work. I used myself up in the accursed "Red Badge."
— STEPHEN CRANE, letter to Curtis Brown, December 31, 1895

1197. I suppose it's easy for anyone to produce their first novel — it's all there inside you and only needs to be written down. . . . After that it becomes more difficult, unless you're prepared to go on writing exactly the same book.
— BARBARA PYM, *Finding a Voice: A Radio Talk*, April 4, 1978

1198. Are these lines really necessary?
— BAYARD TAYLOR, letter to Sidney Lanier, January 12, 1876

1199. The immortal beauty, the immortal goodness of that God, who gives us hands to write, and wits to conceive.
— SIR PHILIP SIDNEY, *Apology for Poetry*, 1595

1200. The novelists are, to be sure, less clear and less precise. But for that very reason they are truer.
— JOSEPH WOOD KRUTCH, "Novelists Know What Philosophers Don't," 1936, in *If You Don't Mind My Saying So*, 1964

1201. Fiction is a work of the imagination, or should be. And the imagination is a faculty that diminished with age.
—MARCIA DAVENPORT, interview, *The New Yorker*, April 22, 1991

1202. I have, I trust, the literary courage to face unbelief.
—FITZ-JAMES O'BRIEN, "What Was It?" *Collected Stories: A Gentleman from Ireland*, 1854

1203. To write a novel is itself such a remarkably hopeful act.
—RICHARD FORD, interview by Roger Bishop in *Book Page*, August 1991

1204. It seems to me that the problem with diaries, and the reason that most of them are so boring, is that every day we vacillate between examining our hangnails and speculating on cosmic order.
—ANN BEATTIE, *Picturing Will*, 1989

1205. There were years in which I could have devoted myself to writing if I had wanted to. It is commonly known that everyone looks back and regrets not following through on more things that mattered to them.
—ANN BEATTIE, *Picturing Will*, 1989

1206. He had tried to write for the wrong reason: to exorcise demons instead of trying to court them and see if, in a fair fight, they won out or the writer did.
—ANN BEATTIE, *Picturing Will*, 1989

1207. I tried an old technique. I would write the demon out of me. Writing had always served as a way of understanding what I was living.
—GAIL SHEEHY, *Passages*, 1976

1208. The fact is that one writes a book not in order to remember it, but in order to forget it.
—THOMAS WOLFE, *The Story of a Novel*, 1936

1209. Of all writings I love only that which is written with blood. Write with blood; and you will discover that blood is spirit.
—FRIEDRICH NIETZSCHE, *Thus Spoke Zarathustra*, 1883

NAME INDEX

SUBJECT INDEX

tor 194; as commodity 121; condemn-
ing 154; and creativity 163; as deed
180; depending on 109; destruction
of 138; and detachment 159; early
1181; edifying 116; empty 88; examination 758; the famous 84;
fascination with 55; fate of 67;
forgotten 106; formative 119; as a
friend 109; genius of a 142; good 26,
84, 94, 103, 105, 107, 134, 138, 139,
151, 172, 195, 564; and happiness 91,
143; historical 524; as history 651;
how to read 151, 306; ill-written 151;
important 119; individuality of 81;
judging 122, 1047; knowledge of
men and 489; law 144; and life 98;
log 757; longest 723; the lost 188;
as a man 1041; mediocre 195; as
messengers 51; as a mirror 123;
misused 110; modern 141, 1057;
must be written 96; and newspapers 27; obscure 152; old 630,
1176; and people 170; political 724;
power of 148; prizes 101; publishing
25, 60, 135, 137, 160, 193; quantity
of 185, 186; rereading 93, 190; revising a 630; sacred 133; scholarly 176;
the second 824; selling 58; sex 86;
significance of 504; source of happiness 77; stolen 113; strangeness of
167; successful 130; summary of our
times 71; tedious 82; title of a 383;
tours 102; travel 198; unread 38;
well-written 151; and women 1104;
as a work of art 180; worst 190;
writing 651; writing itself 819,
850
book column 176
bookshop 29
bookworms 1155
boredom 611
bread 58, 88, 272
brevity 131, 147, 270, 391
Brussels 776
bus 27

career 531, 568, 606, 664, 833, 866,
1189
catastrophe 642, 1019
celibacy 794
censorship 260
chaos 2, 190, 947

character: of an author 47, 504; of a
book 47; and circumstances 703;
congruence of 791; development of
265, 571, 619; dimension of 794; exaggeration 648; feeling for the 878;
heart of a story 919; knowledge of
729; names of a 903; as a puppet 80
characterization 641
characters: author's knowing 789;
author's love for 733; in books 100;
built out of truth 731; creating 635,
727, 731; doubts about 929; dumb
461; as essential 950; evolution of
189; having their own life 100; independence of 681; as independent
beings 585; inner space of 726;
lives of 641; naturalness of 1148; and
politics 724; range of 83; ready-
made 1112; real 47, 916; and real life
persons 856, 870; real people as
510; relationship to the author 589;
speaking 681; tough 639
Chicago 30, 252
child(ren) 68, 113, 136, 157, 200, 203,
306, 424, 440, 536, 553, 611, 626,
816, 883, 886, 964, 967, 997, 999
childhood 19, 201, 494, 668
Christ 143, 177, 713
church 611, 1075
circle 199, 627
civil disobedience 95
civilization 49, 56, 377
clarity 234, 633, 1185
climax 658, 1189
college 114, 225, 234, 659, 863, 886,
987, 1164, 1190
columnists 219
comedy 263, 401, 641, 1019, 1156, 1164
composition 16, 306, 589, 633, 868,
890, 922, 987, 1002, 1081, 1191
computer 517, 997
consciousness 56, 365
conversation 168, 334, 714, 798, 848,
887
cook 17
copyright 401
couplet 343
courage 1007, 1202
craft 239, 611, 779, 844
craftsman 80, 469, 597
criticism 52, 107, 335, 462, 513, 568,
579, 600, 607, 696, 715, 772, 1010,
1011, 1012, 1037, 1111, 1190

genius 142, 522, 607, 647, 752, 753, 784, 982, 1155
genre 184, 704, 830
geography 5
God 30, 33, 36, 104, 138, 237, 272, 319, 416, 466, 498, 555, 567, 627, 645, 654, 697, 722, 728, 746, 860, 875, 958, 1027, 1160, 1199
grammar 233, 243, 253, 625, 1160
grants 338

habit 94, 114, 227, 628, 653, 799, 1012
Hamlet 61, 281, 467
happiness 143, 262, 263, 367
heart 92, 153, 301, 326, 416, 492, 499, 630, 748, 812, 881, 908, 919, 995, 1016, 1031, 1161
hero 8, 80, 506, 870, 922, 929, 1113
heroine 80, 870
historian 325, 524, 1084
histories 651
history 38, 104, 119, 124, 160, 184, 209, 222, 241, 274, 306, 309, 317, 351, 629, 642, 665, 802, 880, 901, 948, 1028, 1173, 1187; oral 665
human experience 306, 327, 951, 1008
human nature 2, 286
human race 45
humor 635, 977, 1007, 1035
hymns 652

idea(s): about books 1021; of animals 233; of an author 80; complexity of 233; distant 345; and essayists 571; and events 292; expression by word 754; expression of language 253; of inspiration 1051; and language 1098; and memories 1103; new 277; odd 92; of a poet 1095; and poetry 369; of publishing 650; scarcity of 1016; translation of 829; and words 469; of a writer 624, 661, 848, 1023; writer's best 733; writer's source of 608; of a writing career 866
idealists 1069
imagination 8, 304, 337, 339, 418, 696, 708, 1026, 1053, 1201
immortality 326
income tax 543
inexperience 41

influence 49, 86, 311, 315, 350, 650, 703
information 350, 478
ink 362, 367, 423, 461, 578, 592, 593, 713, 951, 955, 1022, 1045
inspiration 585, 646, 715, 739, 927, 1051
instinct 438
intelligence 115, 370
interior stance 322
invention 99, 176, 390
inventors 398
Italy 29, 245, 306, 570

journal 192, 249, 350, 392, 435, 538, 556, 557, 583, 584, 658–661, 688, 689, 742, 744, 815, 852, 864, 865, 920, 973, 980
joy 46, 183, 236, 1191

king 158, 265, 319, 568, 719, 756, 764, 788, 816, 967, 1099, 1160, 1161
King Lear 568, 967, 1099
knowledge: expansion of 179; God's 33; hatred of 196; of inner being 948; of life 729; of men 489; preservation of 880; self 568; of a writer 998; and writing 689

language: and ability 243; and advertising 262; and art 255; availability of 247; and censorship 260; chimp 233; civilized 259; clarity of 717; clear 221, 717; common 290; and communication 447; conception of 612; demotic 641; English 225, 231, 244, 251, 254, 263, 572, 1060; evolution of 256, 261; expansion of 236; fancy 1078; fine 221; function of 240; and ideas 1098; innate 233; interaction of 408; limitations of 291; and literature 287, 577; and love 232; and meaning 253, 288, 577; and music 226; and myth 273; nature of 237; organization of 267; and poetry 437; and poets 275, 1161; and power 241; precision of 224; questioning 227; and reason 248; restrictions of 252; and structure 266;